JOHN 3:7

YOU MUST BE BORN AGAIN

by

Maurice Gibney

ORIGINAL WRITING

A catalogue record for this book is available from the British Library and the National Library, Dublin.

978-1-907179-63-1

Published by ORIGINAL WRITING LTD., Dublin, 2010.

Printed by Cahills Printers Ltd

Dedicated to my Lord and Saviour Jesus Christ.

CONTENTS

INTRODUCTION

A man climbing a mountain found himself caught among jagged rocks with a three hundred foot drop below. A helicopter was quickly dispatched to rescue him. After spotting the man in difficulty the rescuers lowered down a rope so the man could strap himself on. But to their utter shock he took no notice of the rope and continued climbing despite the dangerous situation he was in. All of a sudden the man slipped and to the complete horror of his rescuers he plummeted hundreds of feet to his death. Therein lies the difference between a Christian and someone who is religious. However, before we take a closer look at that issue, let me tell you what happened to a friend of mine called Fran. Whilst chatting over a coffee one day Fran told me that he had been sent to Mountjoy prison for failing to pay parking tickets. So I asked him, "Why didn't you just pay them and be done with it?" He told me, "They were just parking tickets, it seemed no big deal at the time." Then he told me, while he was driving into town one day he was stopped by the Garda at a check point and asked to produce his drivers license. After he had given his license to the Garda they called headquarters to see if he had any outstanding convictions. Two hours later Fran found himself in court and as he stood before the judge, he said, "Your honour, I have five hundred euro on me now and I'd like to pay those fines if that's alright?" The judge said, "Listen Mr. Allgood, I'm going to save you that five hundred euro, you're going to prison." Fran got the fright of his life. His big mistake was that he trivialized his crimes by thinking that they were "only" parking tickets, and so he deceived himself. If he had known what the judge was going to say, that he was going to be locked up, he would have made things right between himself and the law a long time ago.

Most of us would have to admit that we have broken God's Law, the Ten Commandments, but it's no big deal. Therefore, let me ask you just a few questions about the Law you have broken to see if it is a big deal. Have you ever told a lie? You may say, "Yes, but only little white lies. They were nothing too serious." Have you ever stolen anything? You may say, "Yes, but nothing huge." Can you see what it is you are doing? You are *trivializing* your crimes, and like Fran, you *will* deceive yourself. What you are really doing is saying that you have not sinned, but the bible warns in 1 John 1:8; If we say that we have no sin, we deceive ourselves, and the truth is not in us NKJV. When the truth is, if you have lied, then you are a liar. If you have ever stolen anything regardless of the value, you are a thief.

What you really need to hear is the judge's ruling for lying and stealing. This is it: "All liars shall have their part in the lake which burns with fire," Revelation 21:8 NKJV. According to God's Law, all liars will end up in hell. You may say that you don't believe in hell but that would be like Fran saying to the judge "I don't believe in jail." What we believe or choose not to believe doesn't change realities. There will not be one thief in heaven, not one (1 Corinthians 6:9). Now take a look at this: Jesus said; "Whoever looks at a woman to lust for her has already committed adultery with her in his heart," Matthew 5:28 NKJV. Have you ever looked with lust? Then you are an adulterer as far as God is concerned. Have you ever used God's name in vain? If the answer is yes and you have either used Jesus' or God's Holy name as a curse word to express disgust instead of using some four letter filth word, you are guilty of blasphemy. This is very serious in God's sight; for the LORD will not hold him guiltless who takes His name in vain, Deuteronomy 5:11 NKJV. If you are honest enough with yourself, you will have to admit that you have broken those Commandments, and therefore you are a self - admitted lying, thieving, blasphemous adulterer at heart and we have only discussed four of the Ten Commandments. If God gives you justice on Judgment Day, you will be found guilty and end up in hell. Think of it, if you were to die today, according to God's Law you would spend eternity in hell. It's not a matter of if you die, but when. It has been estimated that 150,000 people die every day. So what are you going to do about it? How can you make things right between yourself and God's Law? The bible tells us that you are unable to "do" anything. However, God himself has done something amazing to save you from death and hell. He became a person in Jesus Christ and taking your place He suffered and died. He paid the fine in His life's blood for the crimes, *sins* that you have committed. God has demonstrated His love toward us; in that while we were still sinners, Christ died for us, Romans 5:8 NKJV. Then after the third day He rose from the dead defeating death.

Now this is the difference between being religious and being a Christian. There are millions of people in the world who have never seen the serious nature of sin. They are in darkness when it comes to the Judge's final ruling. They have not the slightest idea that they are on their way to hell for crimes which they consider trivial. They understand that they have to face God after they die, but they think that their religious works (like Fran with his five hundred euro) can somehow make payment to get them out of the trouble they are in. So as long as they trivialize their sin, they will deceive themselves into thinking that they can somehow work their own way into heaven by their religious works. But it is as foolish as the man who tried to make it up the mountain by himself, in the end he fell to his death. God Himself has also given to us a rope in the person of Jesus Christ. Only Jesus Christ alone can save us from death and hell, but we must let go of our own efforts to save ourselves and take hold of the rope, which is Christ. The second that we stop our own religious "climbing" and put our faith in Jesus Christ, we find peace with God. It is written in the book of Ephesians chapter 2:8; For by grace are ye saved through faith; and that not of yourselves: *it is* the gift of God: Not of works, least any man should boast KJV. In order to be saved and know it, you must repent and then trust in the Saviour. If you do this, the bible says that God will grant you everlasting life. He will dismiss your case and substitute your death sentence and allow you to live. This is referred to as being, "born again." Jesus said; "Unless one is born again, he cannot see the kingdom of God," John 3:3 NKJV. If you are not born again, you will not enter heaven. If you would like to be born again and be 100% sure that heaven will be your eternal home, please pray something like this.

"Dear God, I confess that I am a sinner. Thank you that Jesus Christ took my punishment upon Himself when He died on the cross at Calvary for my sins. I believe that God raised Him from the dead thereby defeating death. Today I repent and place my trust in Jesus Christ alone for the salvation of my soul. Let your Holy Spirit come into my life now and prepare me for eternal glory. I pray this in Jesus name. Amen."

If you have just prayed this prayer and asked God for His forgiveness, then you have been born again! You have just received the light of God on the inside of you, in your spirit, now you can relate to God. Your relationship with God is personal and He wants to bless you with every spiritual blessing in Christ Jesus. You are now a child of God and are no longer under God's condemnation. Begin to read the bible daily and obey what you read. Jesus said; I have come that they may have life, and that they may have *it* more abundantly, John 10:10 NKJV.

The following chapters will provide you with some insight into the world's most famous book, the bible. I pray that you will enjoy this publication as you discover, many of you for the first time, new facts that will help to build your faith, so you can; always *be* ready to *give* a defence to everyone who asks you a reason for the hope that is in you, with meekness and fear, 1 Peter 3:15 NKJV. God bless you.

CHAPTER I

1. Why do I Need to be Born Again?

The bible teaches that at the beginning of creation God created man in his own image. From the dust of the earth God formed man and breathed into his nostril the breath of life and man became a living soul. God named the first man Adam meaning ground or earth from which he was made. Adam was created as a vessel, his body was made to experience the natural realm, his soul receives knowledge and understanding and his spirit, his inner being was designed for relationship with God. Jesus said that from the beginning of creation God made them male and female. For the reason that a man would leave his father and mother and be united with his wife and the two would become one flesh. Just as there is unity between the Father the Son and the Holy Spirit, God created Adam and Eve to live in unity with one another and with Him.

God gave to Adam headship to represent mankind and provided Adam with the ability to express free will. Having free will enabled Adam to make his own choices and experience love, which without free will is impossible. In order for Adam to freely love God and continue doing good, God gave to him one command that functioned as a test of obedience. This was God's only commandment for both Adam and Eve to keep. However, a day came when they acted independently of God's will and by one sinful act of disobedience they rebelled against God's instruction, thus bringing sin into the world. The penalty for violating God's commandment resulted in Adam and Eve's spiritual death and their progressive physical death. Just as the body without physical life is officially dead, so anyone without spiritual life is described in the bible as being spiritually dead. Therefore the perfect relationship Adam and Eve once had with God was now completely severed.

Genesis 2:7 And the Lord God formed man *of* the dust of the ground, and breathed into his nostrils the breath of life; and man became a living soul. KJV

Matthew 19:4 Have ye not read, that he which made *them* at the beginning made them male and female. KJV

Genesis 2:24 Therefore a man shall leave his father and mother and be joined to his wife, and they shall become one flesh. NKJV

Genesis 2:16 - 17 And the LORD God commanded the man, saying, "Of every tree of the garden you may freely eat; "but of the tree of the knowledge of good and evil you shall not eat, for in the day that you eat of it you shall surely die." NKJV

Romans 5:12 Wherefore, as by one man sin entered into the world, and death by sin; and so death passed upon all men, for that all have sinned. KJV

Genesis 3:20 And Adam called his ˌwife's name Eve; because she was the mother of all living. KJV

Ezekiel 18:4 The soul who sins shall die. NKJV

Acts 17:26 "And he has made from one blood every nation of men to dwell on all the face of the earth, and has determined their preappointed times and the boundaries of their dwellings." NKJV

Psalm 51:5 Behold, I was shapen in iniquity; and in sin did my mother conceive me. KJV

The bible tells us that the fall of mankind took place in the Garden of Eden. Eden had been planted by God east of present day Israel, somewhere in Mesopotamia or Arabia. According to the bible it is from this geological location that the whole human race descended from Adam and Eve. Therefore everyone born of human parents inherits the consequence of Adam's sin. We each have inherited a sin nature thus death continues to affect all of mankind, separating us also from the presence of God.

The final consequence of our sins after we physically die will be eternal separation from God. The good news though, is that God has given mankind the opportunity for reconciliation. The bible says that God gave to the world His only begotten Son Jesus Christ. He was born of a virgin and was without sin, so He could deliver sinful mankind from his wretched state. On the cross at Calvary Jesus Christ gave up His life as a ransom for many. By the shedding of His own blood He became our sinless substitute thus paying our sin debt in full. Through His sacrificial death He satisfied all of God's righteous demands against sin enabling us to be united once again with God. We are told that God offers His saving grace as a free gift to those who repent of their sins and put their trust completely in Jesus Christ. According to the bible it is our confession and belief in the resurrection, plus our commitment to follow Jesus that restores our relationship with our heavenly Father. Our faith in Christ also allows us to escape God's righteous judgment and eternal punishment in hell. Only after a person trusts in Jesus Christ are they truly saved from the penalty and power of sin, thus becoming "born again."

Romans 3:23 For all have sinned, and come short of the glory of God. **KJV**

Ecclesiastes 7:20 For *there* is not a just man on earth who does good And does not sin. **NKJV**

Roman 6:23 For the wages of sin *is* death; but the gift of God *is* eternal life through Jesus Christ our Lord. **KJV**

1 Corinthians 15:22 For as in Adam all die, even so in Christ shall all be made alive. **KJV**

Romans 5:8 But God commendeth his love toward us, in that, while we were yet sinners, Christ died for us. **KJV**

Romans 5:18 Therefore, as through one man's offense judgement came to all men, resulting in condemnation, even so through one Man's righteous act the free gift came to all men, resulting in justification of life. **NKJV**

Hebrews 2:3 How shall we escape if we neglect so great a salvation. **NKJV**

2 Corinthians 6:2 Behold, now *is* the accepted time; behold, now *is* the day of salvation. **KJV**

2. *What Does it Mean to be Born Again?*

In John's gospel, chapter three, there is a remarkable conversation between Jesus and a religious leader named Nicodemus. Nicodemus had come to see Jesus by night to investigate whether or not Jesus was the promised Messiah. He said to Jesus, "Rabbi, we know that you are a teacher who has come from God, for no one can do these miraculous signs that you have been doing unless he is receiving direct help from God." Before Nicodemus had a chance to ask Jesus any questions, Jesus said to him, "I am telling you the truth, unless you are born again you will not see the kingdom of God." Nicodemus asked Jesus, "How can a man be born a second time? Surely he can't enter into his mother's womb and be born, can he?" Jesus answered him and said, "Don't be amazed that I am telling you that you must be born again. That which has been born of the flesh is flesh and that which has been born of the Spirit is spirit." Jesus describes being born from above as a supernatural experience rather than a natural one. In other words, when a woman gives birth to a baby this happens naturally, but he who is born spiritually has been born of God.

In order to become born again we must first come to terms with the knowledge that our sins have separated us from God. When an individual understands that his sin nature is responsible for God's absence in his life, he needs to experience God's mercy and forgiveness. The apostle Paul preached repentance toward God and faith toward Christ, resulting in our justification. When we repent of our sins and place our trust in Christ we automatically pass from death to life. Through faith alone in the atoning work of Christ all of our sins can be forgiven, past, present and future. This is God's unmerited gift of amazing grace which He freely bestows upon repentant sinners. None are worthy or deserving of His grace, nevertheless, we are soundly saved because it. The Holy Spirit carries out the divine work of renewing our spirit by taking residence within our mortal bodies, thus sealing us in Christ. This is God's down payment of our full inheritance to come. The Holy Spirit also

John 3:3 Jesus answered and said to him, "Most assuredly, I say to you, unless one is born again, he cannot see the kingdom of God." **NKJV**

John 3:7 "Do not marvel that I said to you, You must be born again." **NKJV**

John 1:12 - 13 But as many as received him, to them gave he power to become the sons of God, *even* to them that believe on his name: Which were born, not of blood, nor of the will of the flesh, nor of the will of man, but of God. **KJV**

Isaiah 59:2 But your iniquities have separated between you and your God, and your sins have hid *his* face from you, that he will not hear. **KJV**

Romans 10:9 - 10 That if you confess with your mouth the Lord Jesus and believe in your heart that God has raised Him from the dead, you will be saved. For with the heart one believes unto righteousness, and with the mouth confession is made unto salvation. **NKJV**

Ephesians 1:13 - 14 In Him you also *trusted*, after you heard the word of truth, the gospel of your salvation; in whom also, having believed, you were sealed with the Holy Spirit of promise, who is the guarantee of our inheritance until the redemption of the purchased possession, to the praise of His glory. **NKJV**

Romans 8:16 - 17 The Spirit Himself bears witness with our spirit that we are children of God, and if children, then heirs —heirs of God and joint heirs with Christ. **NKJV**

creates within us a new nature whereby allowing our spirit and soul to enjoy Christ's presence in a supernatural way. The broken relationship between us and God is now restored and our new spirit has been made fit for the kingdom of heaven.

After we have become born again the Holy Spirit helps us to renew our minds by giving to us new desires for the things of God, instead of the corruptible things of the world that we were once ensnared to. Old habits begin to slowly fade, like excessive drinking, taking drugs and watching certain programs on TV that are soul destroying. The Holy Spirit confirms to us that we are now Children of God and encourages us to put on Christ. In spiritual terms this means we should begin to set higher moral standards for ourselves instead of the sinful lifestyles we are so accustom to. We have become children of God so it is important to honour God and live our lives according to His will. When we become born again we are not suddenly bound by rules and regulations so that God can spoil our fun. God loves us and wants us to begin making conscious choices that are going to enhance our lives and the lives of those around us. This can only be made possible when we make a definite decision to follow in the footsteps of our blessed saviour Jesus Christ. Being born again is the beginning of a beautiful relationship between us and God, who assures us throughout His word that we are soundly saved and can never be lost again. We are kept safe by God until the day we receive our glorified bodies in the kingdom of heaven.

2 Corinthian 5:17 Therefore, if anyone *is* in Christ, *he is* a new creation; old things have past away; behold, all things have become new. **NKJV**

Romans 13:14 But put on the Lord Jesus Christ, and make no provision for the flesh, to *fulfill its* lusts. **NKJV**

1 Peter 1:23 Having been born again, not of corruptible seed but incorruptible, through the word of God which lives and abides forever. **NKJV**

Romans 12:2 And be not conformed to this world: but be ye transformed by the renewing of your mind, that ye may prove what *is* that good, and acceptable, and perfect, will of God. **KJV**

Romans 6:1 - 2 What shall we say then? Shall we continue in sin that grace may abound? Certainly not! How shall we who died to sin live any longer in it? **NKJV**

John 14:15 If ye love me, keep my commandments. **KJV**

3. Do Good Works Help you to Earn your Salvation?

Although good works are required by God for the Christian to live a godly life, they do not help contribute toward a sinner's justification. The Christian does good works because he is saved not in order to be saved. Genuine repentance and faith in Jesus Christ is all a sinner needs to receive God's forgiveness and free gift of salvation. Repentance is not just being sorry for your sins. True repentance brings about a change of mind, a change of attitude and a change of lifestyle that fits with God's word. Repentance results form expressed grief and remorse when a sinner realises that his sins literally helped in nailing Christ to the cross.

Many believe that they can somehow personally bridge the gap between themselves and God, on the basis of their own personal conduct or performance. Some will even travel the world on pilgrimages or climb mountains in their bare feet in a false belief that an act of penance will purge some of their sins. But according to the bible there is nothing we can do to make atonement for our own sins. If it were possible that we could even pay for just one of our sins, then Jesus died for nothing. Only when we express faith in the finished work of Christ's substitutionary sacrifice on the cross, can God expiate or take away our sins. Our good deeds will only ever measure up as filthy rags in God's sight compared to Christ's perfect atoning work on the cross. That is why we need to trust in the righteousness of Christ. This will lead to eternal life, not our own works of self-righteousness, which will only lead to God's judgment and eternal punishment in hell. Adding anything to the work of the cross demeans the sacrifice of Christ, implying that His complete and finished work wasn't enough.

A rich young ruler once came to Jesus and asked him a serious question. "Good teacher," he said, "what must I do to inherit eternal life?" Jesus graciously and lovingly replied, "Why do you call me good? No one is good but God." Jesus did not retract His own goodness in His reply. His intention

Ephesians 2:10 For we are His workmanship, created in Christ Jesus for good works, which God prepared beforehand that we should walk in them. **NKJV**

2 Corinthians 7:9 - 10 Now I rejoice, not that you were made sorry, but that your sorrow led to repentance. For you were made sorry in a godly manner, that you might suffer loss from us in nothing. For godly sorrow produces repentance *leading* to salvation, not to be regretted; but the sorrow of the world produces death. **NKJV**

2 Corinthians 5:21 For He made Him who knew no sin *to be* sin for us, that we might become the righteousness of God in Him. **NKJV**

Galatians 2:21 "I do not set aside the grace of God; for if righteousness *comes* through the law, then Christ died in vain." **NKJV**

Isaiah 64:6 But we are all like an unclean *thing*, And all our righteousnesses *are* like filthy rags; We all fade as a leaf, And our iniquities, like the wind, Have taken us away. **NKJV**

Romans 4:4 - 5 Now to him who works, the wages are not counted as grace but as debt. But to him who does not work but believes on Him who justifies the ungodly, his faith is accounted for righteousness. **NKJV**

Ephesians 2:8 - 9 For by grace you have been saved through faith, and that not of yourselves; *it is* the gift of God, not of works, lest anyone should boast. **NKJV**

9

was merely to draw out the true condition of this rich young ruler's heart. The young rulers boast was in his own ability at keeping all of God's commandments from his youth.

He was still under the delusion that by keeping God's law he could earn his own salvation. But Jesus said to him, "Sell all you have and give the proceeds to the poor and you will have treasures in heaven, and come, pick up your cross and follow me." When the young man heard this he was grieved because he had many riches and was not willing to part from them. Even though he claimed to have kept God's commandments from his youth, his hidden sin became exposed. His love for his money was far greater than his love for the poor. He had indeed broken God's law after all and went away extremely unhappy because he had made an idol of his wealth.

Though the young ruler claimed to have kept all of God's commandments from his youth, he proved to be just as hypocritical as the Pharisees, who were mainly self righteous religious leaders. In his own self-righteousness he presented himself clean on the outside just like the Pharisees' cups and dishes. Nevertheless, Jesus could see directly into his heart which painted a completely different picture. Jesus said to the Pharisees, "Those who are in good health have no need for a physician, only those who are sick, I did not come for righteous people, I came for sinners." The Pharisees believed they were well, therefore they didn't see their need for a saviour. The tax collectors and prostitutes on the other hand knew that their sins had separated them from God. So they welcomed Jesus' words with open hearts. Jesus embraced them with a love and compassion that this world has not seen since. It was clear that Jesus shared this love for the young ruler but he lacked wholehearted love for God. Jesus offered him eternal life if he would make the sacrifice to give all he had to the poor and follow Him. But his love for his riches overshadowed his love and devotion to God. This deprived him of the greatest treasure of all, an eternity with his creator. For the rich young ruler, it would have been easier

Romans 3:28 Therefore we conclude that a man is justified by faith apart from the deeds of the law. NKJV

Galatians 2:16 Knowing that a man is not justified by the works of the law, but by the faith of Jesus Christ, even we have believed in Jesus Christ, that we might be justified by the faith of Christ, and not by the works of the law: for by the works of the law shall no flesh be justified. KJV

Mark 8:34 - 36 Whosoever will come after me, let him deny himself, and take up his cross, and follow me. For whosoever will save his life shall lose it; but whosoever shall lose his life for my sake and the gospel's, the same shall save it. For what shall it profit a man, if he shall gain the whole world, and lose his own soul? KJV

Matthew 5:20 "For I say to you, that unless your righteousness exceeds *the righteousness* of the scribes and Pharisees, you will by no means enter the kingdom of heaven." NKJV

Matthew 23:25 "Woe to you, scribes and Pharisees, hypocrites! For you cleanse the outside of the cup and dish, but inside they are full of extortion and self-indulgence." NKJV

Mark 2:17 "Those who are well have no need of a physician, but those who are sick. I did not come to call *the righteous*, but sinners, to repentance." NKJV

for a camel to pass through the eye of a needle than for him to have parted with all of his wealth. There is no doubt that those of us who love our material possessions more than Jesus Christ have yet to experience God's grace and forgiveness.

Mark 10:24 - 25 But Jesus answered again and said to them, "Children, how hard it is for those who trust in riches to enter the kingdom of God! It is easier for a camel to go through the eye of an needle than for a rich man to enter the kingdom of God." **NKJV**

Matthew 6:21 "For where your treasure is, there your heart will be also." **NKJV**

4. Who Should I Pray to?

Prayer is the main way in which we develop our relationship with God and should be the most intimate and important activity of our lives. The bible encourages us to pray without ceasing. This does not mean that we should pray every moment of the day, but that we should meditate on things which bring glory to God. God already knows our thoughts and the things we have need of before we even ask Him. Knowing this we should learn how to transform our daily thoughts into daily prayers. This can help strengthen our minds so we can avoid any temptations that may come our way. All of life's temptations begin in the mind, so renewing our minds daily through reading the bible can help us overcome life's struggles and addictions. Certain situations often arise in our lives that make it almost impossible for us to pray and trying to find the right words can often be quite a task. But the Holy Spirit is always aware of our needs and our weaknesses and helps us to find the right words to say during these difficult times.

When the disciples said to Jesus, "Lord, teach us pray," Jesus said to them; "When you pray say; Our Father in heaven, Hallowed be your name," Luke 11:2 NKJV. This prayer was given to the disciples as an introduction or pattern for all their prayers to God. We are told that we should not use vain repetitions like the heathens, for they thought that they would be heard because of their many words. If we are repeating by memory the same words over and over again they just become empty phrases. Prayer is a matter of the heart and we should not be bound by religious obligations which have been set forth for man's approval. Prayer should not be said in a manner which seeks the appraisal of other Christians but with a heart that seeks to please God. Jesus said when you pray you should go into your room and close the door, and when the door is closed, pray to your heavenly Father who hears and sees you in secret and he will reward you openly. The bible is clear that nothing at all should come between us and our communion with God.

1 Thessalonians 5:16 - 18 Rejoice evermore. Pray without ceasing. In every thing give thanks: for this is the will of God in Christ Jesus concerning you. KJV

Philippians 4:8 Finally, brethren, whatever things are true, whatever things *are* noble, whatever things *are* just, whatever things *are* pure, whatever things *are* lovely, whatever things *are* of good report, if *there is* any virtue and if *there is* anything praiseworthy–meditate on these things. NKJV

Psalm 139:4 For *there is* not a word on my tongue, *But* behold, O LORD, You know it altogether. NKJV

James 5:13 - 14 Is anyone among you suffering? Let him pray. Is anyone cheerful? Let him sing psalms. Is anyone among you sick? Let him call for the elders of the church, and let them pray over him, anointing him with oil in the name of the Lord. NKJV

Romans 8:26 Likewise the Spirit also helps in our weaknesses. For we do not know what we should pray for as we ought, but the Spirit Himself makes intercession for us with groanings which cannot be uttered. NKJV

Matthew 6:8 "For your Father knows the things you have need of before you ask Him." NKJV

Hebrews 4:16 Let us therefore come boldly unto the throne of grace, that we may obtain mercy, and find grace to help in time of need. KJV

According to the bible we have only one mediator and that is Jesus Christ. This means only Jesus can stand as a middle man between us and God and no one can approach God in any other way.

The bible describes God as being omnipresent, which means that only God can be everywhere at once. This characteristic can only be attributed to God, as God alone is deity. Therefore it is important to understand that only God can hear and answer our prayers. The bible says that God's ears are always attentive to our prayers and if we ask for anything according to His will, He hears us. Sometimes our prayers may often go unanswered for many years but there may be a very good reason why God has not yet answered. Looking back on my own life I am happy to say I am very thankful to God for many unanswered prayers. Trusting God knows what's best for us is having faith in God's ability to govern our lives, minimising the amount of pain and suffering we might have to endure in times ahead.

Psalm 32:6 For this cause everyone who is godly shall pray to You. **NKJV**

1 Timothy 2:5 For *there is* one God, and one mediator between God and men, the man Christ Jesus. **KJV**

Jeremiah 23:23 - 24 *"Am* I a God near at hand," says the LORD, "And not a God a far off? Can anyone hide himself in secret places, So I shall not see him?" says the LORD; "Do I not fill heaven and earth?" says the LORD. **NKJV**

1 Peter 3:12 "For the eyes of the LORD *are* on the righteous, And His ears *are open* to their prayers; but the face of the LORD *is* against those who do evil." **NKJV**

1 John 5:14 - 15 And this is the confidence that we have in him, that, if we ask any thing according to his will, he heareth us: And if we know that he hear us, whatsoever we ask, we know that we have the petitions that we desired of him. **KJV**

5. Who Should I Trust in for My Salvation?

There are many who have entertained the assumption that all religions ultimately lead to the same God. However, when we examine the exclusive and fundamental teachings of all the world's religions many contradictions soon begin to arise. Even within Christian denominations there exists a false teaching regarding whom we should trust for the salvation of our souls. It is therefore extremely important that we should avoid man made dogmas and religious opinions and look to the bible to investigate the truth concerning our eternal destiny.

In the book of Acts, God's word clearly states that salvation can only be possessed by calling on the name of the Lord Jesus Christ and no one else. According to the bible, trusting in anyone else besides Christ to save you from hell would be a damnable error. As offensive as this may seem to unbelievers the bible's teaching is clear that only through Jesus Christ can forgiveness of sins be possessed. This separates Christianity from all other faith beliefs in the world. For there is no other religion in the world that offers sinners a full pardon from all of their sins before they die through faith alone in a personal saviour.

The bible also teaches us that God has elevated no one else to the role of saviour except His Son Jesus Christ. Nor does anyone else share in God's plan for the redemption of mankind. According to the bible we have only one sinless saviour and that is the Lord Jesus Christ. God could only accept the sinless blood of His Son as a sin offering to make atonement for the sins of the world. This great feat could only be accomplished by Jesus and no one else. Through His death, burial, resurrection and ascension He alone triumphed over Satan making a public spectacle of him by the victory of the cross. Therefore, Jesus Christ's name is above all other names and is the only name you can call upon in order to be saved.

John 14:6 Jesus said to him, "I am the way, the truth, and the life. No one comes to the Father except through Me." **NKJV**

Act 4:12 Neither is there salvation in any other: for there is none other name under heaven given among men, whereby we must be saved. **KJV**

Matthew 1:21 "And she will bring forth a Son, and you shall call His name JESUS, for He will save His people from their sins." **NKJV**

Isaiah 42:8 I *am* the LORD, that *is* My name; And My glory I will not give to another, Nor My praise to carved images. **NKJV**

Isaiah 43:11 I, *even* I, *am* the LORD, And besides Me *there* is no saviour. **NKJV**

Hosea 13:4 "Yet I *am* the LORD your God Ever since the land of Egypt, And you shall know no God but Me; For *there* is no saviour besides Me. **NKJV**

1 Thessalonians 5:9 For God did not appoint us to wrath, but to obtain salvation through our Lord Jesus Christ. **NKJV**

1 John 4:14 And we have seen and do testify that the Father sent the Son *to be* the Saviour of the world. **KJV**

John 3:16 For God so loved the word, that he gave his only begotten Son, that whosoever believeth in him should not perish, but have everlasting life. **KJV**

6. Is Baptism Necessary for Salvation?

Many people believe when they are baptised as infants they automatically become Christians. But baptism in and of itself is not a means of forgiveness nor does baptism take the place of being born again. According to the bible it is the act of repentance and faith alone in Christ that results in our salvation and not the command to be baptised. The bible always emphasises that our sins can only be blotted out by calling on the name of the Lord Jesus Christ and by no other means. Baptism is described as an outward expression of one's inward faith and has nothing at all to do with receiving God's free gift of eternal life.

When Jesus was hanging on the cross, on both His left and right hand side hung two criminals. One of the criminals blasphemed Jesus but the other declared Jesus to be innocent. The one who believed Jesus to be innocent cried out to Him saying, "Lord, remember me when you come into your kingdom," Luke 23:42 NKJV. Jesus didn't say, "quickly take him down off the cross and have him baptised before he passes away." Instead Jesus assured him that, this day, he would be with Him in paradise. This thief was assured of eternal life without ever having to be baptised because he trusted in Jesus Christ. But the other criminal remained condemned because he did not believe that Jesus was who He claimed to be, the sinless Son of God.

In the book of Acts the apostle Philip is seen explaining some verses of prophetic scripture concerning God's Messiah to an Ethiopian eunuch. After the eunuch had heard everything about Jesus of Nazareth he believed that He was truly the Son of God. Then he asked Philip, "What hinders me from being baptised?" Philip replied, "If you believe with all your heart, you may." The eunuch replied, "I believe that Jesus Christ is the Son of God," Acts 8:36 - 37 NKJV. At that moment both Philip and the eunuch went down into the water, where Philip baptised him. The only condition required for the eunuch to be saved is echoed throughout the New Testament. Believe in the Lord Jesus Christ and you

Acts 2:21 And it shall come to pass, *that* whosoever shall call on the name of the Lord shall be saved. **KJV**

Acts 22:16 'And now why are you waiting? Arise and be baptized, and wash away your sins, calling on the name of the Lord.' **NKJV**

Acts 3:19 "Repent therefore and be converted, that your sins may be blotted out, so that times of refreshing may come from the presence of the Lord." **NKJV**

Luke 23:43 And Jesus said to him, "Assuredly, I say to you, today you will be with Me in Paradise." **NKJV**

Mark 16:16 He that believeth and is baptized shall be saved; but he that believeth not shall be damned. **KJV**

John 3:18 He that believeth on him is not condemned: but he that believeth not is condemned already, because he hath not believed in the name of the only begotten Son of God. **KJV**

John 8:24 I said therefore unto you, that ye shall die in your sins: for if ye believe not that I am *he*, ye shall die in your sins. **KJV**

will be saved. This has always been the pattern of first century Christian conversions and the conditions remain the same even today. One must first believe on the Lord Jesus Christ for the forgiveness of his sins before he can be baptised.

When Paul and Silas were in prison in Philippi a great earthquake shook the whole place. Immediately the keeper of the prison awoke from his sleep to find all the cell doors open. Thinking the prisoners had escaped he drew his sword to kill himself but Paul shouted out, "we are all here, don't harm yourself." The jailer then called for a lamp so he could find Paul and trembling with fear he cried out to him, "What must I do to be saved?" Paul gave to him only one answer, "believe on the Lord Jesus Christ and you and your whole household will be saved." The jailer then washed Paul and Silas' wounds and afterwards he plus his whole family were baptised. The members of the jailer's family are not mentioned, but let us keep in mind they had to have been of age in order to understand the gospel and believe in the Lord Jesus Christ. The bible makes no mention of infant baptism here or anywhere else. Everyone in the jailer's household was visibly old enough to believe in Christ.

In the book of Corinthians the apostle Paul actually taught that Christ did not send him to baptise but to preach the gospel. Paul even thanked God that he baptised none. This is no small thanksgiving, for if baptism was indeed necessary for salvation then Paul was thanking God that he saved none. The Lord Jesus Himself also sought not to baptise any, a strange example to leave behind if baptism was necessary for salvation. In fact Jesus declared His own baptism as a work of righteousness. However, the scriptures tell us that salvation is not by works of righteousness which we have done but according to God's mercy He saved us.

Acts 8:36 - 38 Now as they went down the road, they came to some water. And the eunuch said, "See, *here is* water. What hinders me from being baptized?" Then Philip said, "If you believe with all your heart, you may." And he answered and said, "I believe that Jesus Christ is the Son of God." So he commanded the chariot to stand still. And both Philip and the eunuch went down into the water, and he baptized him. NKJV

Acts 16:29 - 31 Then he called for a light, ran in, and fell down trembling before Paul and Silas. And he brought them out and said, "Sirs, what must I do to be saved?" So they said, "Believe on the Lord Jesus Christ, and you will be saved, you and your household." NKJV

1 Corinthians 1:14 - 17 I thank God that I baptized none of you, but Crispus and Gaius; Lest any should say that I had baptized in mine own name. And I baptized also the household of Stephanas: besides, I know not whether I baptized any other. For Christ sent me not to baptize, but to preach the gospel: not with wisdom of words, lest the cross of Christ should be made of none effect. KJV

Matthew 3:15 And Jesus answering said unto him, Suffer *it to be so* now: for thus it becometh us to fulfill all righteousness. KJV

In Caesarea the gentiles received the gift of the Holy Spirit before they were even baptised. This was a clear indication that they had already received remission from sins through their expressed faith and belief in the name of Jesus Christ.

In the book of Romans Paul identifies the new believer as being baptised into Christ Jesus' death. Just as Christ was crucified for our sins and buried, we also are symbolically buried with him in the waters of baptism. The Greek verb *"baptizo"* means to dip or to submerge. This signifies a believer's identity in Christ and his cleansing from sin through Christ's atoning death. Just as Christ was raised from the dead, so it is that we consider ourselves to be dead to sin but alive in Christ Jesus. Our old man, meaning our sin nature, has been crucified once and for all and he can never become un-crucified. Baptism is a testimony of one's inward belief and a convincing that one's sins have truly been washed away. Just as Christ was publicly executed, the new believer makes a public pledge to follow Christ and walk in newness of life.

Titus 3:5 - 7 Not by works of righteousness which we have done, but according to His mercy He saved us, through the washing of regeneration and renewing of the Holy Spirit, whom He poured out on us abundantly through Jesus Christ our Saviour, that having been justified by His grace we should become heirs according to the hope of eternal life. NKJV

Acts 10:43 - 45 "To him all the prophets witness that, through His name, whoever believes in Him will receive remission of sins." While Peter was still speaking these words, the Holy Spirit fell upon all those who heard the word. And those of the circumcision who believed were astonished, as many as came with Peter, because the gift of the Holy Spirit had been poured out on the Gentiles also. NKJV

Romans 6:3 - 4 Know ye not, that so many of us as were baptized into Jesus Christ were baptized into his death? Therefore we are buried with him by baptism into death: that like as Christ was raised up from the dead by the glory of the Father, even so we also should walk in newness of life. KJV

Romans 8:10 And if Christ *be* in you, the body *is* dead because of sin; but the Spirit *is* life because of righteousness. KJV

7. Is the Bible's Interpretation Limited to Only One True Church?

The bible teaches that no one knows the things of God except the Spirit of God. As a man's thoughts are only known to himself so the mind of God is only known by God. The natural man cannot receive the things of the Spirit of God, for they are foolishness to him, nor can he know them because they are spiritually discerned or recognised. In other words, the unrepentant man who is devoid of the Holy Spirit will never have an appreciation for the gospel or good news of salvation unless he is first born again. Only when an unregenerate man receives the gift of the Holy Spirit can he then begin to understand the spiritual content within the bible.

Many well educated men have tried to interpret the bible using their own intellects but the bible is not a book that can be understood through human intellect alone. The bible says that all scripture is given by inspiration of God. This literally means that all scripture is God breathed, therefore, God is their author. As God breathed into Adam's nostrils the breath of life at the beginning of creation, likewise God ministered His word to the apostles as their hearts and minds were moved by the Holy Spirit. The Holy Spirit also helped the apostles to recognise inspired scripture which had been written by other disciples of Jesus Christ. This allowed the apostles to avoid heresy distinguishing truth from error as they constantly abided in God's truth concerning Christ.

When the apostle Paul was referring to all scripture, he was talking about the complete Old Testament as God's inspired truth. Paul also quotes from Luke's gospel in 1 Timothy chapter 5:18 as a reference to scripture. His letters were never addressed to a bishop or select group of leaders but to all Christians at Corinth, Ephesus, Philippi, etc. The apostle Peter also referred to Paul's letters as inspired scripture in 2 Peter chapter 3:16. Paul and Peter's writings plus other close disciples of Jesus Christ like John, make up for nearly all of the New Testament. While they each possessed their own style of writing the Holy Spirit was the one who overruled in their expression of thought and in their choice of words. The same

1 Corinthians 2:11 For what man knows the things of a man except the spirit of the man which is in him? Even so no one knows the things of God except the Spirit of God. **NKJV**

1 Corinthians 2:14 But the natural man does not receive the things of the Spirit of God, for they are foolishness to him; nor can he know *them*, because they are spiritually discerned. **NKJV**

1 Corinthians 2:12 - 13 Now we have received, not the spirit of the world, but the Spirit who is from God, that we might know the things that have been freely given to us by God. These things we also speak, not in words which man's wisdom teaches but which the Holy Spirit teaches, comparing spiritual things with spiritual. **NKJV**

2 Timothy 3:16 All Scripture *is* given by inspiration of God, and *is* profitable for doctrine, for reproof, for correction, for instruction in righteousness. **NKJV**

1 Corinthians 12:7 - 11 But the manifestation of the Spirit is given to each one for the profit *of all*: for to one is given the word of wisdom through the Spirit, to another the word of knowledge through the same Spirit, to another faith by the same Spirit, to another gifts of healings by the same Spirit, to another the working of miracles, to another prophecy, to another discerning of spirits, to another *different* kinds of tongues, to another the interpretation of tongues. But one and the same Spirit works all these things, distributing to each one individually as He wills. **NKJV**

Holy Spirit that inspired the apostles to record and preserve God's word is still at work today helping new believers to understand the bible's content.

The bible says that no prophecy of scripture is of any private interpretation. This scripture has given rise to a number of interpretations such as the false teaching that only learned churchmen can understand the bible's content and only these learned men are able to interpret the bible. Therefore Christians are often told not to study the bible for themselves but to leave it up to the theologians and clergy to interpret God's word for them. However, the bible teaches that Christians are to study the scriptures diligently and test what they read to see if they are in the faith. The ability to understand God's word does not come about through man's intellect alone, but by the impartation of divine revelation from the Holy Spirit. For if the scriptures origin did not come into existence by the will of man but by the will of God, then neither is the scriptures interpretation bound by sinful man's intellect. The bible was given to mankind by God and not to a group of specially trained elite. It is to be a lamp to our feet and a light to all that heed it. Sometimes the bible may be hard to understand but through a personal relationship with Jesus Christ and a deep desire to understand God's word the Holy Spirit will personally guide us into all of God's truth. The ability to interpret and translate the word of God has definitely not been left up to any "one true church" to bestow upon its congregation.

It is important to employ in our interpretation the right methodology. No verse of scripture should be interpreted by itself but in the light of the context and weighed against the rest of scripture. Neither should any personal experience no matter how fantastic hold greater authority than the word of God. The Holy Spirit does not prompt words to substitute the preaching and teaching of the bible nor should modern dogmas or prophetic utterances replace or be compared to the word of God. For many false prophets are at work today, deceiving the minds of those who know not the truth. We should always pray and fast when able in seeking answers from God. Most of all we are to remain faithful to the Lord Jesus Christ and His word.

2 Peter 1:20 Knowing this first, that no prophecy of the Scripture is of any private interpretation. For the prophecy came not in old time by the will of man: but holy men of God spake *as they were* moved by the Holy Ghost. **KJV**

2 Timothy 2:15 Study to show thyself approved unto God, a workman that needeth not to be ashamed, rightly dividing the word of truth. **KJV**

2 Timothy 3:15 And that from childhood you have known the Holy Scriptures, which are able to make you wise for salvation through faith which is in Christ Jesus. **NKJV**

1 John 2:26 - 27 These things I have written to you concerning those who *try to* deceive you. But the anointing which you have received from Him abides in you, and you do not need that anyone teach you; but as the same anointing teaches you concerning all things, and is true, and is not a lie, and just as it has taught you, you will abide in Him. **NKJV**

John 16:13 "However, when He, the Spirit of truth, has come, He will guide you into all truth; for He will not speak on His own *authority,* but whatever He hears He will speak; and He will tell you things to come." **NKJV**

John 14:26 But the Comforter, *which is* the Holy Ghost, whom the Father will send in my name, he shall teach you all things, and bring all things to your remembrance, whatsoever I have said unto you. **KJV**

8. Who is the head of the Church?

When people think of the word church, they normally imagine a huge building made of brick or stone. Although the church is seen as a building in today's world, the bible explains the word church in a different way. The Greek translation of the word church is "*ekklesia*," which means, to be called out or set apart from. This includes all those who have already been saved and redeemed by faith in Jesus Christ. The church should therefore be seen as an organism, an assembly of believers and not an organisation, denomination or hierarchical system. The condition of entrance into the church is based upon ones forsaking of sin and public confession of faith in the Lord Jesus Christ. However, because of the different denominations in the world today, subscription to a creed is often required before new converts are allowed to enter a local congregation. Some creeds can be quite detailed and include general affirmations of faith which are often based upon each individual denominations interpretation of the bible. The bible on the other hand, teaches that only through the preaching of the gospel can sinners be saved and not by adhering to a church creed no matter what denomination it belongs to.

The teaching that the apostle Peter became the "rock" on which Christ would build His church, is a belief held by many today. This belief however, has arisen from the misinterpretation of Matthew's gospel chapter 16:18. Here, Jesus asks His disciples, "Who do people say that I am?" Some of the disciples replied, "Some say John the Baptist, some Elijah, and still others say Jeremiah." Jesus then asked them, "Who do you say that I am?" Simon Peter answered, "You are the Christ the Son of the living God." Jesus replied, "Blessed are you, Simon Bar-Jonah for this has not been revealed to you by flesh and blood, but by my Father who is in heaven; And I also say to you, that you are Peter and on this rock I will build My church, Matthew 16:18 NKJV. If we examine the context of this verse it is important not to lose sight of the revelation that Jesus was God incarnate. It makes no sense whatsoever that Jesus would talk about building His church apart

Galatians 3:8 And the Scripture, foreseeing that God would justify the heathen through faith, preached before the gospel unto Abraham, *saying*, In thee shall all nations be blessed. KJV

1 John 1:9 If we confess our sins, he is faithful and just to forgive us *our* sins, and to cleanse us from all unrighteousness. KJV

Acts 2:44 - 47 Now all who believed were together, and had all things in common, and sold their possessions and goods, and divided them among all, as anyone had need. So continuing daily with one accord in the temple, and breaking bread from house to house, they ate their food with gladness and simplicity of heart, praising God and having favor with all the people. And the Lord added to the church daily those who were being saved. NKJV

Matthew 16:16 - 18 Simon Peter answered and said, "You are the Christ, the Son of the living God." Jesus answered and said to him, "Blessed are you, Simon Bar-Jonah, for flesh and blood has not revealed *this* to you, but My Father who is in heaven. And I also say to you that you are Peter, and on this rock I will build My church, and the gates of Hades shall not prevail against it." NKJV

1 Corinthians 10:4 For they drank of that spiritual Rock that followed them, and that Rock was Christ. NKJV

Isaiah 44:8 Indeed, *there is* no other Rock. NKJV

from what God the Father had just revealed to Peter. Therefore it would be fair to say that the rock on which the church would be built was definitely not Peter. The massive Rock and foundation that the church would be built upon, was Peter's confession, that Jesus was the Christ the Son of the living God. According to the bible, the church is made up of all true believers who acknowledge the deity of Jesus Christ, just as Peter had done. The church is the actual living body of all who agree in mind and spirit with Peter's great confession and this is the foundation of Christ's kingdom.

The apostle Peter never spoke of himself as the foundation of the church, or claimed to be the rock on which it would be built. Instead, Peter portrays the church as a living spiritual house, with the Lord Jesus Christ as the foundation and chief cornerstone and each individual believer as a stone equal to himself. Peter also introduces himself as a fellow elder, a far cry from claiming to be "supreme pontiff" of the church. There is nothing in all of scripture that warrants such an office as the pope. Neither is there any mention of Peter transferring his "power" to a successor. In the book of Acts, when Cornelius fell at Peter's feet and began to worship him, Peter lifted him up saying; "Stand up, I myself also am a man," Acts 10:26 KJV. It would be fitting if all church leaders today would follow Peter's example.

If we trace the figurative use of the word rock through the Old Testament, we discover that it is never used symbolically of man but always of God. The New Testament speaks of only one rock that occupies the place of pre-eminence in the church, the Lord Jesus Christ. According to the scriptures, Jesus Christ is the Rock, foundation and source of growth through whom the whole body of believers are joined and knit together. If Peter was the rock, then according to scripture he was an extremely unstable foundation. When Jesus began explaining to His disciples that He must go to Jerusalem, where He would suffer, be killed and raised on the third day, Peter began to rebuke Him saying, "this shall not happen to you Lord." But Jesus turned to

1 Corinthians 3:11 For no other foundation can anyone lay than that which is laid, which is Jesus Christ. **NKJV**

Romans 1:16 For I am not ashamed of the gospel of Christ: for it is the power of God unto salvation to every one that believeth. **KJV**

1 Peter 5:1 - 2 The elders who are among you I exhort, I who am a fellow elder and a witness of the sufferings of Christ, and also a partaker of the glory that will be revealed: Shepard the flock of God which is among you. **NKJV**

1 Peter 2:6 *"Behold, I lay in Zion A chief cornerstone, elect, precious, And he who believes on Him will by no means be put to shame."* **NKJV**

1 Corinthians 11:3 But I would have you know, that the head of every man is Christ. **KJV**

Psalm 18:31 For who *is* God, except the LORD? And who *is* a rock, except our God? **NKJV**

Ephesians 4:15 - 16 But, speaking the truth in love, may grow up in all things into Him who is the head–Christ– form whom the whole body, joined and knit together by what every joint supplies, according to the effective working by which every part does its share, causes growth of the body for the edifying of itself in love. **NKJV**

Colossians 1:18 And he is the head of the body, the church: who is the beginning, the first-born from the dead; that in all *things* he might have the preeminence. **KJV**

Peter and said; "Get behind Me, Satan! You are an offence to Me," Matthew 16:23 NKJV.

Peter had just denied the very heart of the Christian gospel, declaring that Jesus need not go to the cross. He became a hindrance to Jesus, not being mindful of the things of God and His plan for the redemption of mankind. The means by which mankind would be saved, faith in the substitutionary death of Christ, had just been rejected by the very first "infallible pope." Peter also denied Jesus three times, confirming with an oath that he didn't even know Him. Not wanting to take away from this great apostle but in Matthew chapter 17:4, Peter get's it wrong yet again, when he rashly suggests building three tabernacles as a memorial for Jesus, Moses and Elijah. He was correct in putting Jesus first but wrong when he did not give Him the pre-eminence. This time it is God the Father who rebukes Peter from heaven, saying; "This is My beloved Son, in whom I am well pleased. Hear Him!" Matthew 17:5 NKJV.

When a dispute arose among the disciples as to which of them should be the greatest, Jesus said; "Whoever exalts himself will be humbled, and he who humbles himself will be exalted, Matthew 23:12 NKJV. Jesus reminds His disciples that true greatness is measured in terms of service without thought of reward, reversing the values of the world. While many are seen in today's world as great religious leaders, this was not to be so for Jesus' disciples. No one individual or church was going to be given the power or the authority to lord it over another. The kings who ruled over the gentiles where commonly thought of as great individuals and were even referred to as "benefactors." But this was only a title. The truth is they were generally cruel oppressors who had the appearance of goodness but no distinctive qualities to match. Jesus taught His disciples that it is better to serve than to be served, and giving His life as a ransom for many He led by example the way for all Christians to follow, in giving their own lives to serve others. All the apostles including Paul and Peter recognized that there should be no favouritism among church leaders whatsoever. There should be

Matthew 16:22 Then Peter took him aside and began to rebuke Him, saying, "Far be it from You, Lord; this shall not happen to You!" **NKJV**

Matthew 26:72 But again he denied with an oath. "I do not know the Man!" **NKJV**

Ephesians 1:22 And hath put all *things* under his feet, and gave him *to be* the head over all *things* to the church. **KJV**

Matthew 7:24 "Therefore whoever hears these sayings of Mine, and does them, I will liken him to a wise man who built his house on the rock" **NKJV**

Luke 22:26 "But not so *among* you; on the contrary, he who is greatest among you, let him be as the younger, and he who governs as he who serves." **NKJV**

Matthew 23:8 - 9 "But you, do not be called 'Rabbi'; for One is your Teacher, the Christ, and you are all brethren. Do not call anyone on earth your father; for One is your Father, He who is in heaven." **NKJV**

Luke 9:48 For he that is least among you all, the same shall be great. **KJV**

Romans 2:11 For there is no partiality with God. **NKJV**

Galatians 2:6 But from those who seemed to be something—whatever they were, it makes no difference to me; God shows personal favoritism to no man—for those who seemed *to be something* added nothing to me. **NKJV**

mutual respect among all believers no matter what their denomination or position as long as they are acting in accordance with the word of God.

The apostle Paul describes Christ as being the only foundation on which the prophets and apostles were to build upon. The church is not built on modern dogmas but upon the spiritual heritage handed down to us by the early apostles and prophets of the Christian church. The work of ministry in the church is the undertaking of each member of the body of Christ and not the exclusive charge of chosen leaders. Jesus called some to be apostles, some prophets, some evangelists and some pastors and teachers. Apostles preached the gospel and planted churches. Prophets and prophetess' received direct revelation from God with words of knowledge and wisdom to guide the direction of the church and the saints. Evangelists are men and women that are given the task of converting sinners through using God's law in addressing the sinner's conscience. They would always be ready to give an answer in defence of their faith, encouraging decisions for Christ. Teachers are often unlearned men and women, who are divinely empowered to interpret and explain the word of God. Pastors are men who serve as under-shepherds of the sheep of Christ and are closely related to that of elders. This five fold ministry which Christ gives for the equipping of His church are not for hierarchical control or ecclesiastical competition. God has always used men and women down through the centuries with no previous training, for the nurturing and equipping of the saints who are described throughout the New Testament as Christians.

In Matthew chapter 16:19, Peter is given the keys to the kingdom of heaven. However, Peter was not the only one to receive "the keys to the kingdom of heaven." All the disciples were given the keys to the kingdom of heaven and every born again Christian today is called to carry out the great commission exactly as the apostles were commanded to do. Since we are all taught by the same Holy Spirit we can all possess spiritual discernment as to what God permits and forbids.

Ephesians 2:20 Having been built on the foundation of the apostles and prophets, Jesus Christ Himself being the chief corner*stone.* **NKJV**

Ephesians 4:11 - 12 And He Himself gave some *to be* apostles, some prophets, some evangelists, and some pastors and teachers, for the equipping of the saints for the work of ministry, for the edifying of the body of Christ. **NKJV**

Galatians 3:24 Wherefore the law was our schoolmaster *to bring us* unto Christ, that we might be justified by faith. **KJV**

Matthew 11:25 At that time Jesus answered and said "I thank You, Father, Lord of heaven and earth, that You have hidden these things from *the* wise and prudent and have revealed them to babes." **NKJV**

Acts 20:28 "Therefore take heed to yourselves and to all the flock, among which the Holy Spirit has made you overseers, to shepherd the church of God which He purchased with His own blood." **NKJV**

Matthew 18:17 - 18 "And if he refuses to hear them, tell *it* to the church. But if he refuses even to hear the church, let him be to you like a heathen and a tax collector. Assuredly, I say to you, whatever you bind on earth will be bound in heaven, and whatever you loose on earth will be loosed in heaven." **NKJV**

9. Does Purgatory Exist?

While the bible teaches that Jesus Christ effectively dealt with the whole problem of our sins, there are those who believe the pardoned sinner must still be sent to a place of torment called purgatory for further purification. Purgatory is described as an intermediate state, were departed souls endure expiatory punishment imposed by God to cleanse the sinner from the remnants of sin. While in purgatory a sinner must suffer an unknown degree of punishment for an unknown period of time in order to atone for his own sins. The bible however, never once mentions or even indicates that purgatory exists. Instead the bible points to one whom we can approch and be purified from all sin, the Lord Jesus Christ. Every taint of sin that once offended God can be washed away from those who come to God through faith alone in Christ's atoning blood. This is based upon the complete adequacy of Christ's death on the cross, which was a full propitiatory atonement. The bible says that complete atonement from sin including its punishment is accomplished soley by grace through faith in Christ. There is no "second chance" of atonement after death. Once a person dies without having trusted in Christ, then they will be subject to eternal damnation in hell.

The teaching that Christians must suffer after they die in order to have unrepentant sins purged is purely fictitious. The apostle Paul said, "for me to live is Christ, and to die is gain." Paul also declared that to be absent from the body was to be in the presence of God. If purgatory existed then Paul would have explained his need for further purification before entering into the presence of God, but Paul does no such thing. In fact he states that after having been justified by faith in Jesus Christ we have peace with God.

There are some scripture verses which have also been taken out of context, in an attempt to support the idea of the purging fires in purgatory. One such verse is 1 Corinthians chapter 3:15. Nevertheless, with the help and guidance from the Holy Spirit one can clearly see that 1 Corinthians chapter three

Hebrews 1:3 When he had by himself purged our sins, sat down on the right hand of the Majesty on high. **KJV**

Hebrews 9:14 How much more shall the blood of Christ, who through the eternal Spirit offered himself without spot to God, purge your conscience from dead works to serve the living God? **KJV**

Hebrews 9:27 And as it is appointed unto men once to die, but after this the judgement. **KJV**

Philippians 1:21 - 23 For to me, to live *is* Christ, and to die *is* gain. But if *I* live on in the flesh, this *will mean* fruit from *my* labor; yet what I shall choose I cannot tell. For I am hard-pressed between the two, having a desire to depart and be with Christ, *which* is far better. **NKJV**

2 Corinthians 5:8 We are confident, *I say*, and willing rather to be absent from the body, and to be present with the Lord. **KJV**

Romans 5:1 Therefore being justified by faith, we have peace with God through our Lord Jesus Christ. **KJV**

Colossians 3:15 And let the peace of God rule in your hearts, to which also you were called in one body; and be thankful. **NKJV**

is referring to the judgment seat of Christ where Christian's will themselves be judged according to their works and not their sins. The fire symbolises the testing of each Christian's work or service, of what sort it is. The Christian is already saved despite the fact that his works are consumed by the fire.

The bible teaches that without the shedding of blood there can be no forgiveness of sins. But purgatory isn't said to be a place of blood-shedding, but of "purifying fire." The bible also teaches that only the blood of our sinless saviour can take away, purge or expiate sins not some form of "stigmata" or time spent in purgatory. The teaching of purgatory clearly undermines the work of the cross, by making belief that sinful finite human beings can somehow pay for themselves the infinite penalty demanded by God's justice. However, no amount of suffering in purgatory could ever purge away our sins apart from the spotless blood of our sinless saviour. Only Jesus lived a perfect and sinless life, therefore, only through His blood could forgiveness from sins be made possible. When Jesus shed His own blood on the cross, He effectively purged the sins of everyone who has ever lived, all who are living now, and all who will ever live.

The bible says that God has translated us into the kingdom of his dear Son in whom we have redemption through His blood, the forgiveness of sins. Because of the redemption which is provided by Christ's atoning sacrifice there remains no more an offering left for sins, thus disqualifying the need for any further purification. By the one time offering of Himself, Jesus has perfected forever those who are being sanctified. In other words, the Christian after having been made perfect through faith can now stand before God blameless and free from the guilt and penalty of sin.

Those who believe in the existence of purgatory will nearly always quote from 2 Maccabees chapter 12:38 - 45 as a "proof text." However, this piece of literature is not part of the canon of scripture but can be found among other historical books which

1 Corinthians 3:12 - 15 Now if anyone builds on this foundation *with* gold, silver, precious stones, wood, hay, straw, each one's work will become clear; for the Day will declare it, because it will be revealed by fire; and the fire will test each one's work, of what sort it is. If anyone's work which he has built on *it* endures, he will receive a reward. If anyone's work is burned, he will suffer loss; but he himself will be saved, yet so as through fire. **NKJV**

Hebrews 9:22 And almost all things are by the law purged with blood; and without shedding of blood is no remission. **KJV**

Ephesians 1:7 In whom we have redemption through his blood, the forgiveness of sins, according to the riches of his grace. **KJV**

John 1:29 The next day John seeth Jesus coming unto him, and saith, Behold the Lamb of God, which taketh away the sin of the world. **KJV**

1 John 2:2 And he is the propitiation for our sins: and not for ours only, but also for *the sins of* the whole world. **KJV**

Hebrews 9:26 But now, once at the end of the ages, He has appeared to put away sin by the sacrifice of Himself. **NKJV**

Hebrews 10:14 For by one offering He has perfected forever those who are being sanctified. **NKJV**

Romans 5:9 Much more then, being now justified by his blood, we shall be saved from wrath through him. **KJV**

are known as the Apocrypha or Deutero-canon-icals. These writings were only adopted as scripture by the Catholic Church during the time of the Reformation and Counter-Reformation periods in the sixteenth century. The very word "Apocrypha" comes to us from the Greek word for hidden, or of doubtful authorship. It is important to note that Jesus himself never quoted from any of these apocryphal books and neither did the apostles. The first century Jewish historian Josephus also never used them as scripture. On that authority alone we can say they should never be added to the bible.

The thirty nine books of the Old Testament, excluding the apocryphal books are the only books which were recognized as canonical or accepted as authoritative in Judaism almost since the time of Christ. The 27 books of the New Testament are literally full of Old Testament quotes but none come from these apocryphal books. In the book of 1 Maccabees chapter 9:27 it actually affirms that there were no prophets at this time and so inspiration of God had ceased. Therefore, both the first and second book of Maccabees and other apocryphal books can best be regarded as historical accounts and should not be considered as inspired scripture or used to support any doctrine.

The story line of 2 Maccabees chapter 12:38 - 45 falls under the title of "The sacrifices for the fallen." After a certain battle had been fought it was discovered that the Hebrew soldiers who had fallen in battle were concealing amulets to the idols of Jamnia, which was against Jewish law. This idolatrous sin is recorded as being the reason why these soldiers had fallen in battle. Troubled by this the Jewish general, Judas Maccabaeus, sent money to Jerusalem to offer sacrifices for the deceased soldiers. In doing so Judas was not following the Law of Moses, for according to the scriptures there was no sacrifice that could be offered up on behalf of the dead. It may have been a fine and noble action based upon Judas Maccabaeus belief in the resurrection. But begging forgiveness for someone else's sins by offering up prayers and sacrifices would in no way have helped to purge the sins of these de-

Colossians 1:13 - 14 He has delivered us from the power of darkness and conveyed *us* into the kingdom of the Son of His love, in whom we have redemption through His blood, the forgiveness of sins. **NKJV**

Hebrews 10:18 Now where remission of these *is, there is* no more offering for sin. **KJV**

1 John 2:12 I write unto you, little children, because your sins are forgiven you for his name's sake. **KJV**

1 Peter 1:18 - 19 Knowing that you were not redeemed with corruptible things, *like* silver or gold, from your aimless conduct *received* by tradition from your fathers, but with the precious blood of Christ, as of a lamb without blemish and without spot. **NKJV**

2 Timothy 1:9 Who hath saved us, and called *us* with a holy calling, not according to our works, but according to his own purpose and grace, which was given us in Christ Jesus before the world began. **KJV**

Romans 4:16 Therefore *it is* of faith, that *it might be* by grace. **KJV**

Romans 11:6 And if by grace, then *it is* no longer of works; otherwise grace is no longer grace. But if it is of works, *it is* no longer grace; otherwise work is no longer work. **NKJV**

Galatians 3:11 But that no man is justified by the law in the sight of God, *it is* evident: for, The just shall live by faith. **KJV**

Romans 1:17 For therein is the righteousness of God revealed from faith to faith: as it is writ-

parted soldiers. In all scripture there is no example of Jewish priests or Christians offering up sacrifices or prayers for the dead. These verses contradict the bible's clear teaching that one must first be loosed from their sins by calling on the name of the Lord Jesus Christ before they die. They do not confirm the existence of purgatory or substantiate the teaching of praying for the dead. According to the Bible the sin of idolatry would have landed these soldiers not in purgatory but in hell from which there is no release. Therefore, any prayers said on behalf of the departed is both a waste of time and blasphemous because they make void the full efficiency of Christ's redemptive work on the cross.

The apostle Paul says that we were bought at a price therefore we must honour God with our bodies, which now belong to Him. We have become the purchased possession of God through our Lord and saviour Jesus Christ. The Holy Spirit who is the guarantee of our full redemption places His seal within our very hearts. Therefore, nothing can separate us from the love of God. Christ has redeemed us from the curse of the law by becoming a curse for us. In other words, we broke God's law by sinning, earning our wages which is eternal death but through faith in Jesus Christ we are set free from the very law which condemned us. By becoming our substitute Christ endured the punishment that was due us, therefore setting us free from the curse which the law entailed. The substitutionary death of Jesus fulfilled the righteous demands of God's law, so we are now no longer in bondage to it. We are no longer slaves to sin but slaves of righteousness. The bible says because of Christ's one time sacrifice, salvation is offered to sinners as a free gift, thus disqualifying the need for further purification. Salvation is a free gift which is freely given to repentant sinners who have turned away from their sin towards God's grace, love and abundant mercy.

The Bible sets the Christians heart at rest and gives to him full assurance that eternal life can be possessed before death comes. When Christ died for our sins He accomplished all the work needed for

ten, The just shall live by faith. KJV

Romans 10:13 For whosoever shall call upon the name of the Lord shall be saved. KJV

Romans 6:18 And having been set free from sin, you became slaves of righteousness. NKJV

1 Corinthians 6:19 - 20 Or do you not know that your body is the temple of the Holy Spirit *who is* in you, whom you have from God, and you are not your own? For you were bought at a price; therefore glorify God in your body and in your spirit, which are God's. NKJV

Galatians 3:13 Christ hath redeemed us from the curse of the law, being made a curse for us. KJV

Galatians 4:6 - 7 And because you are sons, God has sent forth the Spirit of His Son into your hearts, crying out, "Abba, Father!" Therefore you are no longer a slave but a son, and if a son, then an heir of God through Christ. NKJV

Ephesians 4:30 And do not grief the Holy Spirit of God, by whom you were sealed for the day of redemption. NKJV

Galatians 5:1 Stand fast therefore in the liberty by which Christ has made us free, and do not be entangled again with a yoke of bondage. NKJV

1 John 5:13 These things have I written unto you that believe on the name of the Son of God; that ye may know that ye have eternal life. KJV

the redemption of our souls. His only request is for all to trust in Him as Saviour and receive spiritual life, thus becoming born again. Having come to Him we can be sure that as far as the east is from the west, so far He has removed our sins from us. We can rejoice because our names have been written in heaven in the Lamb's book of life and we should not be anxious or tossed to and fro by such false teachings as purgatory. God has indicated his acceptance of Christ's sacrifice by raising Him from the dead and by seating Him in heaven at His right hand, where we too are described as being seated in Him.

This expression describes our true spiritual position as a result of our repentance and faith in Christ. We are saved by grace through faith and not by our works, nor by faith plus works but through faith alone in the atoning work of Christ. The work which God the Father had given Jesus to do, the pouring out of His soul as an offering for sin, the atonement and the work of redemption, has provided a way for all sinners to be saved. The work of the cross is a complete and finished work which has already made full provision for sinners everywhere so that anyone who calls upon the name of the Lord will be saved.

Philippians 4:3 And I urge you also, true companion, help these women who labored with me in the gospel, with Clement also, and the rest of my fellow workers, whose names *are* in the Book of Life. **NKJV**

Luke 10:20 "Nevertheless do not rejoice in this, that the spirits are subject to you, but rather rejoice because your names are written in heaven." **NKJV**

Ephesians 2:5 - 6 Even when we were dead in trespasses, made us alive together with Christ (by grace you have been saved), and raised *us* up together, and made *us* sit together in the heavenly *places* in Christ Jesus. **NKJV**

Romans 6:10 - 11 For *the death* that He died, He died to sin once for all; but *the life* that He lives, He lives to God. Likewise you also, reckon yourselves to be dead indeed to sin, but alive to God in Christ Jesus our Lord. **NKJV**

CHAPTER 2

Scientific facts in the Bible

Psalm 19:1
The heavens declare the glory of God. KJV

One of the greatest proofs that the bible is the inspired word of God is the staggering amount of scientific knowledge revealed within scripture. Although the bible's main purpose is not to give scientific information, whenever the bible does touch upon matters relating to science they are stunningly accurate. Through reading the bible one can stumble upon many scientific and medical facts which have been recorded thousands of years before man supposedly "discovered" them. Although these scientific facts are written in a non-scientific language they substantiate and prove the infallibility of God's word. There is no other holy book in any of the world's religions that contains scientific truth. When compared to other ancient writings which abound in the absurd it becomes impossible to explain away the bible's claim to have been supernaturally inspired by God. It's always wise to consider the evidence presented before making a decision on whether or not something is true. Since the truth cannot contradict itself we should naturally expect the bible to be in harmony with observable science. To the contrary, not one single scientific discovery has ever discredited a biblical statement. Through reading the following scripture verses you will soon discover that the bible in no way separates God from the scientific study of His creation.

1. The Earth Suspended in Space

Thousands of years ago it was believed that the earth rested upon a large animal or giant. In Greek mythology it was the god Atlas who is seen holding the earth upon his shoulders. But written almost 3,500 years ago in the book of Job chapter 26:7 the bibles states; He (God) stretcheth out the north over the empty place, *and* hangeth the earth upon nothing KJV. Amazingly Job describes the earth as being suspended in space. This poetic depiction of the earth's position and movement in the solar system is an amazing statement of scientific fact. Sir Isaac Newton did not publish his Universal Theory of Gravitation until 1687.

2. The Bible Reveals the Earth is Globe Shaped

At a time when the rest of the world believed that the earth was flat, the bible informs us that the earth is round. It is written in the book of Isaiah chapter 40:22; *It is* He (God) who sits above the circle of the earth, And its inhabitants *are* like grasshoppers NKJV. This does not mean the compass of the horizon as critics often claim, but the circular of the earth as a globe shaped object. The bible also supports a spherical earth in other scripture verses. In the book of Job chapter 26:10 the earth is described as if being in motion, as day and night occur both simultaneously. Also in Job chapter 38:14 God uses a figurative expression of a clay vessel being rotated upon a potter's wheel as an analogy of the earth's rotation.

Job 22:14
Thick clouds cover Him, so that He cannot see, And He walks above the circle of heaven. **NKJV**

Job 26:10
He hath compassed the waters with bounds, until the day and night come to an end. **KJV**

Job 38:14
It is turned as clay *to* the seal. **KJV**

3. The Bible and Oceanography

Matthew Maury (1806-1873) an officer who served in the United States Navy is considered the father of oceanography and hydrography. While reading his bible one day he noticed in the book of Psalms chapter 8:8 the expression, "paths of the seas." Maury enthusiastically set out to discover whether or not these paths actually existed. Because of Maury's belief in the scriptures his research led him to the discovery of the ocean's paths of warm and cold continental currents. Today Maury is known as the path finder of the seas. His book; The Physical Geography of the Sea and Its Meteorology, was the first on oceanography and is still referred to in many universities. The book of Psalms mostly authored by King David was written between 1000 - 300 B.C. Remarkably God revealed this revelation to King David who had probably never even seen the ocean.

4. The Springs of the Sea

In the book Job chapter 38:16 God challenges Job to answer some remarkable questions; "Have you entered the springs of the sea? Or have you walked in search of the depths?" NKJV. The springs of the sea were not discovered until the 1970's when oceanographers ventured to the dark ocean's floor in research submarines built to withstand 6,000 pounds per square inch of immense water pressure. Under water cameras attached to these submarines revealed to oceanographer's hot water vents on the ocean's floor. It would have been virtually impossible for Job to have explored the ocean's floor and for him to have discovered these under water springs for himself. This striking revelation was revealed to Job more than 3,500 years ago.

Proverbs 8:28
When he established the clouds above: when he strengthened the fountains of the deep. **KJV**

5. Mountains and Valleys at the Bottom of the Ocean

Many critics have alleged that the prophet Jonah was a mythical person and mock the fact that Jonah was taken down into the depths of the sea in the stomach of a great sea monster. However, the critics have failed to read the full story. When Jonah was taken down into the depths of the sea in the belly of this great fish, it is suggested that he may have actually died. The bible records Jonah as crying out to God from the depths of hell, which in the Hebrew is "*Sheol.*" This is the great pit in the centre of the earth where the souls of those who have not trusted in Christ are kept awaiting the resurrection and the final judgment. During Jonah's decent into the abyss he describes the mountains at the bottom of the sea and how the foundation of the sea floor had closed in behind him. The Lord Jesus referred to Jonah's experience when he predicted his own death and resurrection as a sign to an evil and adulterous generation in Luke's gospel. Jonah's description of the bottom of the deep and the reality of hell could have played a major roll in the repentance of over one hundred and twenty thousand people in the city of Nineveh. Only in recent years has man discovered that there are valleys and under water mountain ranges along the ocean's floor. The Atlantic Ocean contains an undersea range of mountains stretching ten thousand miles long. The massive Mariana's trench in the Pacific Ocean is up to six and a half miles deep. If you put Mount Everest inside, the peak would still be a mile below the water's surface. How did Jonah know what the ocean's floor looked like if he had not of been an eye witness? The answer is obvious. About 700 B.C. God revealed this revelation to the prophet Jonah which stands as a remarkable sign of repentance for the human race today as the second coming of Jesus Christ draws near.

Jonah 2:6
I went down to the bottoms of the mountains; the earth with her bars *was* about me forever: yet hast thou brought up my life from corruption, O LORD my God. **KJV**

Matthew 12:40
"For as Jonah was three days and three nights in the belly of the great fish, so will the Son of Man be three days and three nights in the heart of the earth." **NKJV**

Luke 11:29 - 30
And when the people were gathered thick together, he began to say, This is an evil generation: they seek a sign; and there shall no sign be given it, but the sign of Jonah the prophet. For as Jonah was a sign unto the Ninevites, so shall also the Son of man be to this generation. **KJV**

6. *The Hydrologic Cycle*

Thousands of years ago the ancients would have observed many rivers flowing into the oceans but they had no understanding as to why the sea level did not rise. Amazingly the bible reveals to us the earth's complete hydrological cycle of evaporation, cloud formation and precipitation. It is written in the book of Ecclesiastes chapter 1:7; All the rivers run into the sea, Yet the sea *is* not full; To the place from which the rivers come, There they return again NKJV. This bible verse and other similar scriptures clearly speak of the earth's hydrologic cycle, a fact which has only been discovered and scientifically confirmed by modern meteorologists.

Amos 9:6
He who builds His layers in the sky, And has founded His strata in the earth; Who calls for the waters of the sea, And pours them out on the face of the earth– The Lord *is* His name. **NKJV**

Job 36:27 - 29
For He draws up drops of water, Which distill as rain from the mist, Which the clouds drop down *And* pour abundantly on man. Indeed, can *anyone* understand the spreading of the clouds, The thunder from His canopy? **NKJV**

Job 37:16
Do you know how the clouds are balanced? **NKJV**

7. The Bible and the Spreading of Disease

Only centuries ago it was common practice for a doctor to perform an autopsy on the body of a deceased woman. Then without washing his hands he would go straight into the maternity ward and examine expectant mothers. This was considered normal medical practice because unknown to these doctors was the presence of microscopic germs which transported deadly diseases. The Encyclopaedia Britannica documents that in 1845 a doctor named Ignaz Semmelweis from Vienna ordered all doctors and medical students to wash their hands with chlorinated lime under running water before and after examining all patients. Immediately the death rate dropped from 30 percent to less than 2 percent. Thousands of years before modern science discovered micro organisms, God gave advanced medical knowledge to His people. It is written in the book of Leviticus chapter 15:13; 'And when he who has a discharge is cleansed of his discharge, then he shall count for himself seven days for his cleansing, wash his clothes, and bathe his body in running water; then he shall be clean' **NKJV**. These laws regarding sanitation were also carried out if anyone came into contact with a dead animal or human being. Even pottery which sustained cracks was to be broken and thrown away. We can note that not until recent years was the washing of hands under running water taught as a safety measure to help stop the spreading of infection. Doctors would have normally washed their hands in bowls of water leaving invisible germs on their hands which would have resulted in the death of multitudes. How could God's people have known that the precautions they were taking by washing their flesh and clothes in running water was preventing the spread of serious bacterial infections? This practice was well in advance and far exceeded that of the Egyptians and other ancient societies of its day.

8. The Bible and Biology

It is written in the book of Leviticus chapter 17:11; For the life of the flesh *is* in the blood: and I have given it to you upon the altar to make an atonement for your souls: for it *is* the blood *that* maketh an atonement for the soul KJV. This verse of scripture indicates that the blood, both in symbol and in reality is the life source of the body and soul. Blood circulation is the key element in physical life a discovery made by William Harvey in 1616. Blood is a liquid tissue consisting of 55 percent plasma (a yellowish fluid that contains proteins) and 45 percent blood cells. Suspended in the plasma are red and white blood cells. Blood has two main functions, transport and defence. The red blood cells contain haemoglobin, which transports oxygen and carbon dioxide. The white blood cells protect the body against infection. Platelets also help the blood clot when a wound occurs. The blood carries water and nourishment to every cell and maintains body temperature. As we can see the blood is the very key and breath to life itself and there is no greater way of describing the body's function than to say, "The life of the flesh is in the blood."

9. The Bible and the Immune System

According to the Old Covenant God directed Abraham to circumcise all male newborn babies on the eighth day. Why the eighth day? Medical science has recently discovered that between the fifth and seventh day of the newborn babies' life, vitamin K coupled with prothrombin reaches its peak. These specific factors in the blood help prevent haemorrhaging and allow the blood to clot quickly. The eighth day therefore is the optimum day for an operation as the human body's immune system is also at its peak. The scientific knowledge found in the bible proves yet again how advanced the Hebrew people had become under God's guidance.

Genesis 17:12
And he that is eight days old shall be circumcised among you, every man child in your generations. **KJV**

Leviticus 12:3
And in the eight day the flesh of his foreskin shall be circumcised. **KJV**

10. Man Created From the Dust of the Earth

It is written in the book of Genesis chapter 2:7; And the Lord God formed man *of* the dust of the ground and breathed into his nostrils the breath of life; and man became a living soul KJV. For years critics have ridiculed the simplicity of God's supernatural creation of man from the dust of the ground. But modern

34

science has since revealed to us that every single element within the human body can also be found in the dust of the earth. The most common element of these is oxygen, being the most abundant element on the earth's crust or on the ground; it makes up 65% mass of the human body. Carbon 18 %, Hydrogen 10%, Nitrogen 3.3%, Calcium 1.5%, Phosphorous 1.2%, Potassium 0.2% and Sulphur 0.2%. The biblical summary for the creation of life works out exactly as God had foretold. Moses being the author of the first five books of the bible called the Torah would have had absolutely no idea that the earth contained any of these elements.

Genesis 3:19
"In the sweat of your face you shall eat bread. Till you return to the ground, For out of it you where taken; For dust you *are*, And to dust you shall return." **NKJV**

Job 10:9
Remember, I pray, that You have made me like clay. And will You turn me into dust again? **NKJV**

11. The Treasury of the Snow

It was not until the invention of the microscope that man discovered each and every snowflake was a unique symmetrical treasure. Snowflakes are formed when water vapour in the air cools and condenses into drops of water, each drop of water then freezes into a tiny ice crystal smaller than a pin hole. The size and shape of each snow crystal depends mainly on the temperature of their formation and the amount of water vapour available at deposition. There is an infinite variety of snowflakes and just like human fingerprints no two are alike. This remarkable treasure of creation has gone unnoticed for thousands of years. But these snow crystals were no secret to God when he asked Job; Hast thou entered into the treasures of the snow? Job 38:22 KJV

12. Creation, the Bible and Atoms

The bible claims that the whole of creation is made of invisible material. It is written in the book of Hebrews chapter 11:3; Through faith we understand that the worlds were framed by the word of God, so that things which are seen were not made of things which do appear KJV. Energy is indiscernible and so are atoms, molecules and gases to the naked eye, yet combined they become visible.

Two thousand years ago science would have been ignorant of the subject but the bible agrees perfectly that the entire creation was made of invisible elements called "atoms."

Colossians 1:16
For by him (Christ) were all things created, that are in heaven, and that are in earth, visible and invisible, whether *they be* thrones, or dominions, or principalities, or powers: all things were created by him, and for him. **KJV**

Romans 1:20 - 21
For the invisible things of him from the creation of the world are clearly seen, being understood by the things that are made, *even* his eternal power and Godhead; so that they are without excuse. Because that, when they knew God, they glorified *him* not as God, neither were thankful; but became vain in their imaginations, and their foolish heart was darkened. **KJV**

13. The Bible and Dinosaurs

According to evolutionists, dinosaurs first evolved around 235 million years ago but around 65 million years ago they became extinct because of some sort of cataclysmic event. Theories like these are taught to children and adults worldwide in order to make belief the idea of millions of years. However, evolutionists obtain their dates by indirect dating methods which other scientists often dispute. The bible on the other hand teaches that all land dwelling animals were created on day six of the creation week including dinosaurs around six thousand years ago. Adam and Eve were also created on day six, so according to the bible dinosaurs lived alongside man. Many people claim that the word dinosaur cannot be found in the bible. But the word dinosaur, meaning "terrible lizard," was not invented until 1841 by a man named Sir Richard Owen, a British anatomist and first superintendent of the British Museum. The bible refers to these terrible lizards as "dragons" which fit accurately with scripture. There are many dragon legends from around the world, with many descriptions of these dragons that fit the characteristics of specific dinosaurs. The bible describes many unique and amazing creatures. One in particular was called "behemoth" which means "huge beast." In the book of Job it says; "Look now at the behemoth, which I made *along* with you; He eats grass like an ox. See now, his strength *is* in his hips, and his power *is* in his stomach muscles. He moves his tail like a cedar; The sinews of his thighs are tightly knit. His bones *are like* beams of bronze, His ribs like bars of iron. He *is* the first of the ways of God" Job 40:15 - 19 NKJV. Behemoth was the largest of all the land dwelling animals which God had created. His tail is compared to a large cedar tree and he is described as having the capacity to drink up rivers while remaining undisturbed by the rivers raging current. This description fits perfectly with that of a brachiosaurus. These 50 ton creatures were among the largest animals to have walked the earth and there is no mystery surrounding their disappearance. God just allowed them to become extinct; Only He who made him can bring near His sword, Job 40:19 NKJV.

There has always been strong evidence throughout history to support the fact that man and dinosaur co-existed. In approximately A.D. 1186 the Ta Prohm temple near Siem Reap Cambodia was built by King Jayavarman VII. Many unique carved statues and stone columns fill the temple-monastery. One particular carved image is that of a very convincing Stegosaurus. In South Eastern Utah in the U.S. one of the third largest natural bridges in the world, Kachina Bridge, holds a petroglyph which looks exactly like a large Sauropod dinosaur. It is believed to be the work of the Anasazi Indians who once lived in the region between A.D. 700 - 1250. Also in Utah's black dragon canyon a very large pictograph of a winged creature can be found with a crest on its head and what looks like webbed feet. When the Indians drew this thunder bird like picture they did not draw feathers on its wings. Amazingly fossil bones of pterodactyls have been discovered in black dragon canyon. In the Havasupai Canyon Northern Arizona in the U.S. there is a particular rock wall which also shows a figure cut into the sandstone. The figure is standing upright and balanced upon its own tail, a given indication that the artist must have seen it alive. Many unbiased paleontologists agree that this petroglyph reveals a long necked long tailed and wide bodied dinosaur. Another interesting discovery was made on the floor of Carlisle Cathedral in Cumbria England. The Cathedral was founded in the 12th century and contains the tomb of a 15th century bishop named Richard Bell. His tomb is inlaid with brass which shows engravings of two animals that resemble sauropod dinosaurs. Amazingly these engravings and paintings are only hundreds of years old and there is no recollection of man reconstructing dinosaur fossils until the middle of the 19th century. There also exists physical evidence that dinosaur fossils are not millions of years old. The discovery of un-fossilized "fresh" dinosaur bones found on the North Shore of Alaska went unnoticed for twenty years. This discovery was not reported because the bones were assumed to be that of bison and not dinosaurs. These bones should not have looked and felt like old cow bones if they were really 65 million years old. In 1990 at the University of Montana scientists discovered T. Rex bones that were partially un-

37

fossilized. Sections of these bones were like fresh bone and when examined the shocking discovery of red blood cells was made. If these bones where really millions of years old then the blood cells and haemoglobin would have completely disintegrated. The latest fossil to produce amazingly well preserved soft tissue is a salamander allegedly "18 million years old." Its muscle tissue is supposedly the most pristine example yet among the many others which stand as remarkable evidence that man did indeed co-exist with dinosaurs just as the bible reveals.

Psalm 91:13
Thou shalt tread upon the lion and adder: the young lion and the dragon shalt thou trample under feet. **KJV**

Isaiah 30:6
Into the land of trouble and anguish, from whence *come* the young and old lion, the viper and fiery flying serpent. **KJV**

Isaiah 43:20
The beast of the field shall honour me, the dragons and the owls. **KJV**

Jeremiah 14:6
And the wild asses did stand in the high places, they snuffed up the wind like dragons; their eyes did fail, because *there was* no grass. **KJV**

14. Time, Space, Matter and Creation

A basic scientific principal called "the law of causality," states that no effect can be greater than its cause. Everything that exists must be the result of a previous cause. For the evolutionist the universe began with a "big bang." This was caused by elementary particles of matter which evolved out of nothing! From this cosmic explosion came all life. The bible on the other hand expresses the universe in five terms; time, space, matter, power and motion. This revelation was given to Moses, the author of the first five books of the Old Testament called the Torah or in Greek the Pentateuch. In the beginning (time), God created (power), the heavens (space), and the earth (matter), and the Spirit of God moved (motion), upon the face of the waters. Maybe God made space three dimensional to remind us of his unique triune nature. God is three in persons and yet he is also one in nature. The name *"Elohim,"* which is the Old Testament name for the divine "Godhead," is plural in form with its Hebrew *"im"* ending describing the triune God and creator of this tri-universe. Time is also a sort of three-in-one with the past, present and the future. As Christians we remember the past as we partake of the bread and wine in the present, while looking forward to the Lord's second coming in the future. Time has been fused with meaning as we await the coming of our Lord Jesus Christ. The evolutionist who denies the existence of God will argue, on the one hand that, complex systems of ordered life and their artistic design, such as human beings, came into existence by meaningless random chance. Then, on the other hand, will expect us to believe that each mutation toward that first step of man's evolution was meaningful. However, macroevolution is nothing more than meaningless blind theory. There is no scientific evidence to show that macroevolution has ever occurred and no mutation has ever been observed that adds a little information to the genome. So what do we really see when we look at the complexity of life? We see creation, design, art and order. If everything else in the world has a creator, a designer, an artist and order behind it, why would we rule out the fact that there is a Creator, a Designer, and an Artist behind the ordered universe? An orderly universe testifies to the greatest statement ever spoken and the law of causality simply points to the one who made this statement possible, "in the beginning, God" Genesis 1:1 KJV

Genesis 1:1 - 2
In the beginning God created the heaven and the earth. And the earth was without form, and void; and darkness *was* upon the face of the deep. And the Spirit of God moved upon the face of the waters. **KJV**

CHAPTER 3

Manuscript Evidence

2 Peter 1:16
For we have not followed cunningly devised fables, when we made known unto you the power and coming of our Lord Jesus Christ, but were eyewitnesses of his majesty. **KJV**

Are the New Testament gospels the true eyewitness history of the life of Jesus Christ or has the story been changed down through the centuries? Must we simply take the New Testament's history concerning Jesus of Nazareth by faith and commit intellectual suicide? Or is there firm historical evidence to support the reliability of the gospels? Critics often point out that the New Testament was written so long ago that nobody can know for sure it hasn't been tampered with down through the centuries. However, the truth is we can and do know that the New Testament hasn't been changed through the science of textual criticism. Basically the more texts we possess the less doubt there is concerning the original and when it comes to the New Testament we have a great wealth of material. In fact there are over 5,500 Greek manuscripts containing all or part of the New Testament, over 10,000 in Latin and 9,300 in other languages, a total of nearly 25,000 manuscript copies or portions of the New Testament in existence today. The second largest collection of manuscript testimony next to the New Testament is of Homer's Iliad. Composed about 800 B.C. there are only 643 surviving Greek manuscripts. The earliest copies, some quite fragmentary, have come down to us from the second and third century A.D. a very lengthy time gap of a thousand years. Aristotle wrote his poetics around 343 B.C. and yet the earliest known copy to date is A.D. 1100 a time gap of almost fourteen hundred years, with only five manuscripts in existence. Consider Caesar's Gallic War, composed between 58 - 50 B.C. we have only nine or ten good copies, the oldest written some 900 years later than Caesar's day. The history of Herodotus 480 - 425 B.C. is known to us from only eight manuscripts, the earliest belonging to A.D. 900 and the same can be said of the History of Thucydides 460 - 400 B.C. Yet no classical scholar would question the credibility of these works in spite of the large time gaps and the much smaller collection of available manuscripts. The fact remains that there is no other document of antiquity which even approaches the New Testaments textual availability and integrity.

Papyrus findings have also thrown plenty of light on the authenticity of the New Testament. The Chester Beatty Biblical Papyri are a group of early papyrus manuscripts of biblical texts which were purchased in the 1930's from a dealer in Egypt. They contain nearly all the New Testament books, including portions of the four gospels, the book of Acts, large portions of Paul's Epistles and the book of Revelation. They have been dated between A.D. 200 - 250. The Bodmer Papyri are another collection of important manuscripts which include Old and New Testament texts and writings of the early churches. They were purchased by Martian Bodmer of Switzerland from a dealer in Egypt during the 1950's and have been dated to around A.D. 200 and earlier. One of the earliest surviving pieces of New Testament Scripture is a fragment of papyrus codex called the Ryland's Papyrus. This papyrus also found in Egypt is located today at the John Ryland's Library in Manchester, England. It has been dated between A.D. 117 - 138 and contains five verses of scripture from the gospel of John chapter 18:31 - 33 and verses 37 - 38, which records part of Jesus' trial before Pontius Pilate. In 1955 a fragment of papyrus known as 7Q5 was discovered in a cave along the west shore of the Dead Sea. It has been dated between A.D. 50 - 60 and is strongly believed by many papyrologists to be a fragment of Mark's gospel chapter 6:52 - 53. According to Jose O'Callaghan a world renowned papyrologist, nine other New Testament fragments were discovered in the same cave which had been sealed closed since A.D. 68. In 1994 Orsolina Montevecchi one of the greatest papyrologists of our time and Honorary President of the International Papyrologist Association, stated concerning the fragment, "I do not think there can be any doubt about the identification of 7Q5."

These manuscripts plus many more add to the overwhelming historical evidence of the New Testament. In comparison with other historical literature there is no great period between the events of the New Testament and the New Testament writings. Nor is there any great time lapse between the apostles' original writings and the oldest currently existing manuscripts. Textual critics both Christian and non Christian have agreed that the text of the New Testament is almost exactly as it was originally written. The parts which are debatable are extremely minor and in no way affect basic Christian doctrines. This wealth of extant manuscript evidence proves beyond a doubt that the New Testament says precisely the same things today as it originally did almost two thousand years ago. When the books of the New Testament were composed many of the authors were actual eyewitnesses or an associate to an eyewitness of the Lord Jesus Christ. One thing we can definitely be sure about is that the apostles were not telling handed down legends. The bottom line is when compared to other ancient writings of antiquity the New Testament stands unapproachable.

CHAPTER 4

The Life of Jesus Foretold Through Prophecy

John 13:19
"Now I tell you before it comes, that when it does come to pass, you may believe that I am *He*." **NKJV**

When it comes to bible prophecy there is no other religious book or writings in the world that contain specific, repeated, and unfailing prophecies. These predictions were made hundreds of years in advance of events over which the prophet had absolutely no control. Muslims, Hindus, and Buddhists have their own sacred holy books, but all are without the element of proven prophecy. However, contained within the Old Testament are over 300 distinct prophecies that describe the coming and passing of God's Messiah. These predictions were written centuries before Jesus Christ was born by men from different backgrounds and languages, yet the portrayal of Jesus of Nazareth is completely consistent with all of the Old Testament's Messianic prophecies. Through a close study of these unique prophecies we can easily establish Jesus' divine credentials and identifiably confirm His Messiahship.

For many years there has been much rejection as to the authenticity and credibility of the Old Testament's Messianic prophecies. Scholars at one time took these prophecies lightly, maintaining that the prophecies concerning the Messiah were probably written long after the advent of Christ and inserted into the Old Testament. Apart from having no proof to support this theory, this view is no longer accepted by any critic of the bible today since the remarkable archaeological discovery of the Dead Sea Scrolls. The Dead Sea Scrolls were first discovered by a Bedouin shepherd who stumbled upon them in what was to be the first of a total of 11 caves. This discovery was made along the northwest shore of the Dead Sea at Qumran in 1947. Scholars have since identified the remains of more than 800 separate scrolls written mostly in Hebrew, a smaller number in Aramaic and a few in ancient Greek. The scrolls were apparently hidden by a strict sect of Jews called the Essenes. It is believed that the Essenes may have brought the scrolls to the caves for safekeeping before the first Jewish Revolt against the Romans in A.D. 70. They are the oldest group of Old Testament manuscripts in existence and include one complete Old Testament book of Isaiah and thousands of fragments representing every Old Testament book except Ester.

The scepticism evoked by the discovery of the Dead Sea Scrolls caused them to be subjected to the most rigorous of all examinations. As a result their genuineness has been well established. The book of Isaiah, referred to as the Isaiah Scroll, has been dated by paleographers to be between 175 and 125 B.C. This outdates any previous known copy of Isaiah by up to one thousand years, confirming to us the reliability and authenticity of the book of Isaiah that we possess in our bibles today. These manuscripts stand as remarkable corroborating evidence in support of the Old Testament scriptures and can be used as a powerful tool for answering textual critics. The Dead Sea Scrolls also serve to us the earliest window found so far into the history of Old Testament texts on predictive prophecies.

There are still many critics that will only accept Jesus as being a good teacher and not the Christ, regardless of the prophetic evidence provided. These critics claim that Jesus purposely fulfilled many of the Messianic prophecies recorded in the Old Testament, in order to substantiate His claims to Messiahship. Apart from this being contrary to Jesus' honest character, it makes Him out to be hypocrite and a liar. After all, Jesus personally declared that it was He of whom Moses and the prophets spoke about. This could not be the Jesus these same critics accept as only a good teacher, if He was indeed trying to fulfil these prophecies in order to deceive people. He would not be a good teacher after all but nothing less than an evil deceiver. Besides, many of the prophecies which Jesus fulfilled were completely outside of his control. These include His place of birth, the soldiers who cast lots for His garments, His side being pierced by the soldier's spear and His place of burial. The fact that these four prophecies were literally fulfilled by Jesus in one 24 hour period should be evidence enough for any sceptic. Nevertheless, Jesus not only fulfilled these four prophecies on the day that he was crucified but an amazing twenty five specific prophecies. Now according to the laws of probability, the chances of these twenty five predictions coming to pass in one twenty four hour period of Jesus' lifetime must be billions to one.

It is willingly admitted that many "prophecies" concerning Christ are not completely predictive. Some scholars say that the New Testament writers related specific Old Testament passages to Christ that were not directly predictive of Him. Many scholars speak of these Old Testament texts as being "topologically fulfilled" in Christ. In other words, some truth in the verse is appropriately applied to Christ, even though it was not directly predictive of Him. However, others speak of a common meaning in the Old Testament verse, that applies to both its Old Testament reference (Israel) and the New Testament reference (Christ), both of whom were God's "Son." A number of scholars portray this as a double-reference view of prophecy. Many Old Testament verses on the other hand, are not simply typological but are visibly predictive, such as the time and place of Jesus' birth and death. In conclusion the bible is literally filled with specific predictive prophecies that have clearly been fulfilled in the person of Jesus Christ. These fulfilled prophecies unfailingly stand as superior evidence that Jesus Christ is the unique Son of God and demonstrate to us the tremendous credibility of the bible, a truth that many will soon come to discover through a rigorous examination of the following evidence.

To help compare the record of Old Testament prophecies and their New Testament fulfilment I have placed 39 of the Old Testament's prophecies concerning the Messiah above its New Testament fulfilment. The first ten prophecies concern the birth, ministry and resurrection of Jesus. The subsequent 29 prophecies were fulfilled in the last 24 hours of Jesus' life. Commentary concerning these prophecies can be found in between both the prophecy and its fulfilment. Please keep in mind that these prophecies were fulfilled within the time frame of Jesus' birth, not before 2 B.C. and His death, which was no later than A.D. 33.

Prophecies Concerning Jesus Life, Ministry and Resurrection

1. Born of the Seed of Woman

PROPHECY DATE: About 1440 B.C.
Genesis 3:15
"And I will put enmity Between you and the woman, And between your seed and her Seed; He shall bruise your head, And you shall bruise His heel." NKJV

This prophecy is often referred to as the first Messianic prophecy in the Old Testament. The Seed of the woman is a reference to a future descendant of Eve who would have no human father namely the Messiah. Jesus Christ fulfilled this prophecy when He was born of the virgin Mary and He would crush the Devil's head spelling his ultimate defeat. The woman's Seed Messiah would be bruised, this happened at Calvary when Jesus was crucified. When sin entered the world, the serpent became the first to fall victim to God's curse. Whatever may have been the serpent's former glory this creature's Devil possessed body would now

44

crawl on its belly covered in the dust of shame. However, we are told that at Christ's second coming everything will be returned to its former glory just as it was before the curse took place in Eden.

FULFILLMENT
Galatians 4:4
But when the fullness of the time was come, God sent forth his Son, made of a woman, made under the law. **KJV**

2. Born of a Virgin

PROPHECY DATE: About 700 B.C.
Isaiah 7:14
Therefore the Lord himself shall give you a sign; Behold, a virgin shall conceive, and bear a son, and shall call his name Immanuel. **KJV**

This verse points to Jesus Christ the promised Messiah of whose birth and life were announced long before Mary was born. Critics in their attempts to discredit the virgin birth often state that the Hebrew word for virgin can also mean young woman or maiden. However, the Greek word in the New Testament *"parthenos,"* is used only when describing a young woman who is a pure virgin. The teaching that Mary remained a virgin her whole life holds no foundation in scripture. We are told in the gospel of Matthew chapter 1:25 that Joseph did not have any sexual relations with Mary till or until she had given birth to Jesus. This verse shows that the consummation of their marriage would have taken place after Jesus had been born in obedience to the will of God as recorded in Genesis chapter 2:24; Therefore a man shall leave his father and mother and be joined to his wife, and they shall become one flesh NKJV. Joseph and Mary are recorded as being a normal husband and wife well up until Jesus had reached the age of twelve. If Joseph and Mary where living a celibate married life it would have been in rebellion against God's perfect will. A celibate marriage for twelve years would have also been completely unnatural and unheard of. The bible states that after the birth of Christ, Mary had other children and makes very clear the distinctions between Jesus' own brothers, brethren and relatives including His cousins.

FULFILLMENT
Luke 1:26 - 27, 30 - 31
Now in the sixth month the angel Gabriel was sent by God to a city of Galilee named Nazareth, to a virgin betrothed to a man whose name was Joseph, of the house of David. The virgin's name *was* Mary. V 30 - 31; Then the angel said to

45

her, "Do not be afraid, Mary, for you have found favour with God. And behold you will conceive in your womb and bring forth a Son, and shall call His name JESUS." **NKJV**

3. Born in Bethlehem

PROPHECY DATE: About 700 B.C.
Micah 5:2
But thou, Bethlehem Ephratah, *though* thou be little among the thousands of Judah, *yet* out of thee shall he come forth unto me *that is* to be Ruler in Israel; whose goings forth *have been* from of old, from everlasting. **KJV**

The prophet Micah predicts the precise birthplace of the Messiah. He points to Bethlehem Ephratah, which is in Judah six miles south of Jerusalem. Even the unbelieving Jewish scribes identified this as a prophecy concerning the birth of the Messiah and directed the inquiring magi or wise men to Bethlehem. Bethlehem, meaning the house of bread, became the birthplace of Jesus Christ, the one who would call Himself the Bread of Life. Though the Messiah's lineage could be traced back to His royal ancestor David, His origin goes all the way back to eternity.

FULFILLMENT
Luke 2:4 - 7
And Joseph also went up from Galilee, out of the city of Nazareth, into Judea, unto the city of David, which is called Bethlehem; (because he was of the house and lineage of David :) To be taxed with Mary his espoused wife, being great with child. And so it was, that, while they were there, the days were accomplished that she should be delivered. And she brought forth her firstborn son, and wrapped him in swaddling clothes, and laid him in a manger, because there was no room for them in the inn. **KJV**

4. Preceded by a Messenger

PROPHECY DATE: About 450 B.C.
Malachi 3:1
Behold, I will send my messenger, and he shall prepare the way before me: and the Lord, whom ye seek, shall suddenly come to his temple, even the messenger of the covenant, whom ye delight in: behold, he shall come, saith the LORD of hosts. **KJV**

This prophecy seen it's fulfilment in the appearance of John the Baptist who was God's messenger and forerunner to Christ's First Advent.

FULFILLMENT
Luke 7:24, 27
When the messengers of John had departed, He began to speak to the multi-tudes concerning John: "What did you go out into the wilderness to see? A reed shaken by the wind?" V 27; "This is *he* of whom it is written: '*Behold, I send My messenger before Your face, Who will prepare Your way before You.*' NKJV

5. Enter Jerusalem on a Donkey

PROPHECY DATE: About 500 B.C.
Zechariah 9:9
Rejoice greatly, O daughter of Zion; shout, O daughter of Jerusalem: behold, thy King cometh unto thee: he *is* just, and having salvation; lowly, and riding upon an ass, and upon a colt, the foal of an ass. **KJV**

The Prophet Zechariah describes to us in detail that this King would come in lowly grace riding on a donkey into Jerusalem. This is historically referred to as the "triumphal entry." Jesus of Nazareth rode through the city on a carpet of palm branches up to the Eastern Gate where He entered the Temple Mount. Mul-titudes had turned out to greet Him shouting "Hosanna," which means, save us now. Jesus was in no doubt declaring Himself to be the promised Messiah. This day is known to us as Palm Sunday and it is celebrated annually throughout the world. Critics have been known to point to Matthew's gospel chapter 21:7 and say that Matthew was in error because he recorded Jesus riding or sitting upon "two" donkeys. However, on close inspection we see Matthew explaining that Jesus was set upon the coats which were set upon both donkeys. Common sense and the scriptures tell us that Jesus came riding on the foal of an ass which was not yet broken, meaning, no one had yet rode upon and it may have still been following its mother. So both donkeys would have been brought, the foal and its mother to ride along side, keeping control over her young. The fact that no one had ever ridden the foal is of special significance.

FULFILLMENT
Mark 11:7 - 11
And they brought the colt to Jesus, and cast their garments on him; and he sat upon him. And many spread their garments in the way: and others cut down branches off the trees, and strewed *them* in the way. And they that went before, and they that followed, cried, saying, Hosanna; Blessed *is* he that cometh in the name of the Lord: Blessed *be* the kingdom of our father David, that cometh in the name of the Lord: Hosanna in the highest. And Jesus entered into Jerusalem, and into the temple: and when he had looked round about upon all things, and now the eventide was come, he went out unto Bethany with the twelve. **KJV**

6. *Perform Miracles*

PROPHECY DATE: About 700 B.C.
Isaiah 35:5 - 6
Then the eyes of the blind shall be opened, and the ears of the deaf shall be unstopped. Then shall the lame *man* leap as a hart, and the tongue of the dumb sing. **KJV**

While John the Baptist had been imprisoned by Herod he became discouraged and began to let doubt get the better of him. Like many great men of God, John suffered a momentary lapse of faith, so he sent two of his disciples to Jesus to question whether or not He was truly the Messiah. Jesus affirmed His Messiahship to John's disciples by quoting a verse of scripture that would have been very familiar to John. This would have brought great comfort and reassurance to John just before Herod had him put to death.

FULFILLMENT
Matthew 11:4 - 5
Jesus answered and said unto them, Go and show John again those things which ye do hear and see: The blind receive their sight, and the lame walk, the lepers are cleansed, and the deaf hear, the dead are raised up, and the poor have the gospel preached to them. **KJV**

7. *Saviour to both Jews and Gentiles*

PROPHECY DATE: About 700 B.C.
Isaiah 49:6
Indeed He says, 'It is too small a thing that You should be My Servant To raise up the tribes of Jacob, And to restore the preserved ones of Israel; I will also give You as a light to the Gentiles, That You should be My salvation to the ends of the earth.' **NKJV**

According to God's plan of redemption, Jesus was set apart to die on the cross for us before the creation of the world. Jesus, who existed with God in the beginning, stepped out from eternity to become the living incarnate God and mankind's saviour. Having been rejected by the Jewish nation He would become a light of salvation to the gentile nations of the world.

FULFILLMENT
Acts 13:47 - 48
"For so the Lord has commanded us: *'I have set you as a light to the Gentiles, That you should be for salvation to the ends of the earth.'* " Now when the Gentiles heard this, they were glad and glorified the word of the Lord. And as many as had been appointed to eternal life believed. **NKJV**

8. Shall be Judge

PROPHECY DATE: About 700 B.C.
Isaiah 2:4
And he shall judge among the nations, and shall rebuke many people: and they shall beat their swords into plowshares, and their spears into pruninghooks: nation shall not lift up sword against nation, neither shall they learn war any more. **KJV**

This prophecy indicates the rule and reign of Christ in the world to come where there will be no more bloodshed and a cessation of war and evil. Judgment will come for all unbelievers at Jesus' second advent. Only those whose names have been written in the Book of Life will escape eternal damnation in hell.

FULFILLMENT
John 5:30
I can of mine own self do nothing: as I hear, I judge: and my judgment is just; because I seek not mine own will, but the will of the Father which hath sent me. **KJV**

9. Raised from the Dead

PROPHECY DATE: 1000 - 300 B.C.
Psalm 16:10
For thou wilt not leave my soul in hell; neither wilt thou suffer thine Holy One to see corruption. **KJV**

The bible teaches that Christ entered into hell and while there, He proclaimed his victory over Satan to all the demon spirits who are in chains while awaiting the final judgment. God then raised Jesus from the dead preventing his body from decomposition. After witnessing Christ's resurrection the disciples received the keys to the kingdom of heaven. If someone was bound by sin or indwelt by a demon they could be loosed from their sin through the preaching of the gospel and the demons would be exorcised. The disciples did not receive the power to absolve people's sins. Forgiveness of sins was preached in Jesus' name and those who accepted Jesus Christ as their personal saviour received forgiveness of sins. Those who rejected Christ remained condemned and their sins would be retained for the final judgment.

FULFILLMENT
Acts 2:31 - 32
He seeing this before spake of the resurrection of Christ, that his soul was not left in hell, neither his flesh did see corruption. This Jesus hath God raised up, whereof we all are witnesses. **KJV**

10. Ascension into Heaven

PROPHECY DATE: 1000 - 300 B.C.
Psalm 68:18
You have ascended on high. **NKJV**

As soon as Jesus had commissioned His disciples, He was taken up into heaven where He is seated at the right hand of God in full majesty and authority. The fact that Jesus sat down indicates the posture of rest from His finished and complete sacrificial work of redemption. Unlike the Old Testament priests who had to continuously offer ineffective animal sacrifices, Jesus having finished His New Covenant work on Calvary sat down forever being uninterrupted because sin's tremendous claim has been settled forever.

FULFILLMENT
Acts 1:9
And when he had spoken these things, while they beheld, he was taken up; and a cloud received him out of their sight. **KJV**

The next twenty-nine prophecies were spoken at various times by many different prophets between 1000 - 500 B.C. All of these prophecies were literally fulfilled in Jesus in one twenty-four hour period of time.

1. Betrayed by a Friend

PROPHECY DATE: 1000 - 300 B.C.
Psalm 41:9
Even my own familiar friend in whom I trusted, Who ate my bread, Has lifted up *his* heel against me. **NKJV**

This psalm, although written in combination with David's cabinet member Ahithophel in 2 Samuel, matches the life and death of Judas Iscariot. When Jesus identified Judas Iscariot as His betrayer at the last supper he omitted the words "my own familiar friend in whom I trusted." Knowing already that Judas was going to betray Him, Jesus simply said, *'He who eats bread with Me has lifted up his heel against Me,'* John 13:18 NKJV

FULFILLMENT
Matthew 10:4
Judas Iscariot, who also betrayed Him. **KJV**

2. *Betrayed for Thirty Pieces of Silver*

PROPHECY DATE: About 500 B.C.
Zechariah 11:12
And I said unto them, If ye think good, give *me* my price; and if not, forbear. So they weighed for my price thirty *pieces* of silver. **KJV**

According to the Mosaic Law, thirty shekels of silver was the price of a good slave. It was also the price prophesied by the Prophet Zechariah which would be delivered into the hands of Jesus' betrayer Judas Iscariot. Judas informed the high priests where they could arrest Jesus without being surrounded by a large gathering of Jesus' followers.

FULFILLMENT
Matthew 26:15
What will ye give me, and I will deliver him unto you? And they covenanted with him for thirty pieces of silver. **KJV**

3. *Silver to be thrown into God's House 4. Silver Used to buy Potter's Field.*

PROPHECY DATE: About 500 B.C.
Zechariah 11:13
And the LORD said to me, "Throw it to the potter" –that princely price they set on me. So I took the thirty *pieces* of silver and threw them into the house of the LORD for the potter. **NKJV**

This prophecy was fulfilled after Judas Iscariot betrayed Jesus, and the silver did indeed go to the purchasing of the potter's field. Judas reached a point of regret for betraying Jesus but never repented. Instead his guilt led him to take his own life.

FULFILLMENT
Matthew 27:5 - 7
And he cast down the pieces of silver in the temple, and departed, and went and hanged himself. And the chief priests took the silver pieces, and said, It is not lawful for to put them into the treasury, because it is the price of blood. And they took counsel, and bought with them the potter's field, to bury strangers in. **KJV**

5. *Forsaken by His Disciples*

PROPHECY DATE: About 500 B.C.
Zechariah 13:7
Awake, O sword, against my shepherd, and against the man *that* is my fellow, saith the LORD of hosts: smite the shepherd, and the sheep shall be scattered: and I will turn mine hand upon the little ones. **KJV**

This prophecy clearly speaks of God's servant the Messiah as the good shepherd. Jesus clearly portrayed Himself as the good shepherd who would lay down His life for His sheep. The sword of God's justice would strike Jesus Christ at Calvary for the sins of the world and the sheep, the disciples (Israel) would be scattered. God's hand would later turn to the aid of the disciples after Christ's resurrection through the indwelling power of His Holy Spirit. Though they deserted Christ at the time of his arrest and crucifixion, after witnessing his resurrection they later became fearless ministers of the gospel which eventually cost them their own lives.

FULFILLMENT
Mark 14:50
And they all forsook him, and fled. **KJV**

6. *Accused by False Witnesses*

PROPHECY DATE: 1000 - 300 B.C.
Psalm 35:11
False witnesses did rise up; they laid to my charge *things* that I knew not. **KJV**

In finding an excuse to put Jesus to death, false witnesses were brought before the Jewish leaders during His mock trial. They distorted Jesus' teaching about His resurrection and accused Him of threatening to destroy the temple. Finally they accused Him of blasphemy demanding that he be put to death.

FULFILLMENT
Matthew 26:59 - 60
Now the chief priests, and elders, and all the council, sought false witness against Jesus, to put him to death; But found none: yea, though many false witnesses came, *yet* found they none. At the last came two false witnesses. **KJV**

7. *Silent before His Accusers*

PROPHECY DATE: About 700 B.C.
Isaiah 53:7
He was oppressed, and he was afflicted, yet he opened not His mouth. **KJV**

Although Jesus could have made rightful accusations against all who oppressed Him He opened not His mouth but willingly submitted to all the humiliation and suffering for us. Pilate marvelled at how Jesus did not utter one scornful word against those who wanted Him dead. Most if not all prisoners that stood guilty before Pilate would have tried to profess their innocence to avoid the death sentence. The apostle Philip, one of the twelve disciples, explained this verse of scripture to the Ethiopian eunuch, in the book of Acts, as he led him into a personal relationship with the Lord Jesus Christ.

FULFILLMENT
Matthew 27:12
And when he was accused of the chief priests and elders, he answered nothing.
KJV

8. Wounded and Bruised

PROPHECY DATE: About 700 B.C.
Isaiah 53:5
But he *was* wounded for our transgressions, *he was* bruised for our iniquities: the chastisement of our peace *was* upon him; and with his stripes we are healed.
KJV

Jesus suffered blows by a rod, the Roman scourging, a crown of thorns placed on His head, nails in His hands and feet and a spear thrust into His side, all for our sins. He was bruised and crushed for our wickedness and rebellion. The chastisement for our peace was upon Him. In other words, the punishment which we deserve for our own sins fell completely upon Christ. By His stripes we are healed, meaning, through the cross we can claim victory over death.

FULFILLMENT
Matthew 27:26
Then released he Barabbas unto them: and when he had scourged Jesus, he delivered *him* to be crucified. KJV

9. He Was Hated Without Cause

PROPHECY DATE: 1000 - 300 B.C.
Psalm 69:4
They that hate me without a cause are more than the hairs of mine head. KJV

The multitudes that greeted Jesus with shouts of, "Hosanna, Blessed is He who comes in the name of the Lord," where now shouting "crucify Him." This unruly mob hated Jesus through their deliberate choice. God knowing that this would happen caused King David, the earthly ancestor of the promised Messiah, to write it down. This same hate for Jesus continues today as Christians are persecuted worldwide in countries such as China, North Korea, Indonesia, Philippians, Pakistan, Afghanistan, Iran, Turkey and mostly all other Muslim and communist countries. If Jesus were alive today he would be rejected twice as much because the world's deeds have become more evil and men love darkness rather than light.

FULFILLMENT
John 15:25
But *this cometh to pass,* that the word might be fulfilled that is written in their law, They hated me without a cause. **KJV**

10. *Struck and Spat Upon*

PROPHECY DATE: About 700 B.C.
Isaiah 50:6
I gave my back to the smiters, and my cheeks to them that plucked off the hair: I hid not my face from shame and spitting. **KJV**

They spat in Jesus' face and plucked out His beard, the only perfect and sinless man who ever lived. His visage or appearance was marred beyond recognition as a man to the astonishment of many bystanders. With all the shame and humiliation, Jesus' naked and battered body hung on the cross to make atonement for our sin debt. Jesus willingly gave Himself over to the suffering and shame knowing that God would vindicate Him and all who would come to Him through repentance and faith in His resurrection.

FULFILLMENT
Matthew 26:67
Then they spat in His face and beat Him; and others struck *Him* with the palms of their hands. **NKJV**

11. *Mocked and Ridiculed*

PROPHECY DATE: 1000 - 300 B.C.
Psalm 22:7 - 8
All those who see Me ridicule Me; They shoot out the lip, they shake the head, *saying,* "He trusted in the LORD, let Him rescue Him; Let Him deliver Him, since He delights in Him!" **NKJV**

This is precisely what the jeering crowd said as Jesus hung on the cross. Incredibly nothing has changed today as Christians are often mocked by the secular media in regards to Christ's second coming. But the Lord is not slack concerning His promises. God is patient toward us, not willing that anyone should perish but that all come to repentance. Unfortunately not all will be saved, for the road to destruction is wide and well travelled as many choose to live their lives apart from the will of God.

FULFILLMENT
Matthew 27:29
And when they had plaited a crown of thorns, they put *it* upon his head, and a reed in his right hand: and they bowed the knee before him, and mocked him, saying, Hail, King of the Jews! **KJV**

12. *People Would Shake Their Heads at Him*

PROPHECY DATE: 1000 - 300 B.C.
Psalm 109:25
I became also a reproach unto them: *when* they looked upon me they shaked their heads. **KJV**

Those who looked upon Jesus wagging their heads blasphemed Him. "Save yourself," they shouted, "if you are the Son of God." But if Jesus had of miraculously come down from the cross then all of mankind would have been destined for hell. God could only accept a perfect sinless sacrifice to make atonement for the sins of the world and only Jesus Christ could meet God's demands. When Christ died on the cross a divine transaction was made, a sinless life for a sinful world. Christ's sacrificial work on the cross allows all who trust in Him to stand righteous before a Holy and just God.

FULFILLMENT
Matthew 27:39
And those who passed by blasphemed Him, wagging their heads. **NKJV**

13. *They Would Stare Upon Him*

PROPHECY DATE: 1000 - 300 B.C.
Psalm 22:17
I can count all My bones, They look *and* stare at Me. **NKJV**

After Jesus had been bound He was delivered to Pontius Pilate who had Him scourged. Tied to a post sticking out from the ground Jesus would have been beaten without mercy. A leather whip consisting of several leather thongs each attached with jagged pieces of metal or bone and weighed at each end with led would have ripped fragments of flesh from Christ's body. This horrendous form of torture was known as "half way death." As Jesus' blood covered body hung on the cross His bones would have literally been visible for Him to count and for those who stared intently at Him.

FULFILLMENT
Luke 23:35
And the people stood looking on. **NKJV**

14. He Would Fall Under The Cross

PROPHECY DATE: 1000 - 300 B.C.
Psalm 109:24
My knees are weak through fasting; and my flesh faileth of fatness. **KJV**

Because Jesus became so weak under the weight of the cross His knees gave way falling hard on the ground. So the soldiers compelled a man named Simon of Cyrene to carry the cross for Jesus. There is not much known about Simon but the scriptures suggest that his two sons Alexander and Rufus became well known Christians.

FULFILLMENT
John 19:17
And he bearing his cross went forth into a place called *the place* of the skull, which is called in the Hebrew Golgotha. **KJV**

15. Executed With Thieves

PROPHECY DATE: About 700 B.C.
Isaiah 53:12
And he was numbered with the transgressors. **KJV**

As Jesus was set between the two thieves on the cross they hurled insults at Him. But then one of the thieves had a dramatic change of heart. Perhaps on hearing Jesus pray for those who wanted Him dead opened the thief's spiritual eyes to God's infinite love and mercy. Turning to Jesus the thief cried out, "Lord remember me when You come into your kingdom." **Luke 23:42 NKJV** This was certainly a death bed repentance that paid off, as Jesus replied to him, "Assuredly, I say to you, today you will be with Me in Paradise," **Luke 23:24 NKJV**

FULFILLMENT
Matthew 27:38
Then were there two thieves crucified with him, one on the right hand, and another on the left. **KJV**

16. They Pierced His Hands and Feet

PROPHECY DATE: 1000 - 300 B.C.
Psalms 22:16
For dogs have surrounded Me; The congregation of the wicked has enclosed Me. They pierced My hands and My feet. **NKJV**

While on the cross Jesus was surrounded by "dogs," a term used for evil doers and unbelieving gentiles. Here it refers particularly to the Roman soldiers who pierced His hands and feet, a clear reference to the nails which affixed Jesus to the cross. The burning pain of the nails hitting the median nerve in His wrists would have exploded up His arms into His brain and down His spine. Jesus would have suffered exhaustion, shock, lockjaw, dehydration and paralysis as He hung on the cross. According to Jewish criminal law crucifixion was unheard of until the Romans adopted and incorporated it as a form of punishment for criminals hundreds of years after this prophecy had been made.

FULFILLMENT
Luke 23:33
And when they had come to the place called Calvary, there they crucified Him. **NKJV**

17. Pray for His Persecutors

PROPHECY DATE: About 700 B.C.
Isaiah 53:12
And He bore the sin of many, And made intercession for the transgressors. **NKJV**

If you were asked, what has Jesus Christ's death got to do with you? What would be your reply? You may well believe that Jesus' death has nothing at all to do with you, that he died two thousand years ago long before you were even born.

But the fact is that we have all played a part in the death of Jesus Christ. We have all sinned, and Jesus paid the price for those sins. When Jesus made intercession for us this means more than just prayer. Christ gave himself completely on behalf of mankind. His work of intercession began on the cross and it continues today as God's free gift of salvation is offered to sinners worldwide.

FULFILLMENT
Luke 23:34
Then said Jesus, Father, forgive them; for they know not what they do. **KJV**

18. His Friends and Family Stood Afar Off

PROPHECY DATE: 1000 - 300 B.C.
Psalm 38:11
My loved ones and My friends stand aloof from my plague, And my relatives stand afar off. **NKJV**

Even though the apostle Thomas at one time said to his fellow disciples; "let us also go, that we may die with him," John 11:16 KJV and Peter exclaimed, "I will lay down my life for thy sake," John 13:37 KJV. Only John and the Lord's mother Mary stood close by as Jesus hung on the cross. Jesus instructed John to take care of Mary as if she were his own mother. It is noticeable that Jesus called His mother "woman," not in disrespect, but like at the wedding in Cana, Jesus used the term woman in regard to Mary's rank. Mary was never to be placed in a position where she would be adored. Remember, Jesus obeyed and did only what He saw His Father doing, He followed the Father's timing, not the commands of His own family.

FULFILLMENT
Luke 23:49
And all his acquaintance, and the women that followed him from Galilee, stood afar off, beholding these things. **KJV**

19. His Garments would be Divided and Gambled For

PROPHECY DATE: 1000 - 300 B.C.
Psalm 22:18
They divide My garments among them, And for my clothing they cast lots. **NKJV**

Another prophecy within this unique Psalm deals with the Roman soldiers who divided Christ's garments among themselves and cast lots for His clothing. This is referred to in all four Gospels concerning Christ's garments which the soldiers divided into four and His tunic which was without seam, they cast lots for. Little did they know that they were fulfilling a prophecy which had been written a thousand years before their mindless actions.

FULFILLMENT
John 19:23 - 24
Then the soldiers, when they had crucified Jesus, took his garments, and made four parts, to every soldier a part; and also *his* coat: now the coat was without seam, woven from the top throughout. They said therefore among themselves, Let us not rend it, but cast lots for it, whose it shall be: that the Scripture might be fulfilled, which saith, They parted my raiment among them, and for my vesture they did cast lots. These things therefore the soldiers did. **KJV**

20. He Would Suffer Thirst 21. Gall and Vinegar would be offered to Him

PROPHECY DATE: 1000 - 300 B.C.
Psalm 69:21
They also gave me gall for my food, And for my thirst they gave me vinegar to drink. **NKJV**

Gall was a bitter poisonous herb which was used to make a painkilling substance. Jesus was offered a drink containing gall but refused to drink it even though He was in excruciating agony. He would not drink it because He had to suffer in our place on the cross in full consciousness. Those who mocked Jesus also offered up to Him sour wine on a sponge. These were not acts of mercy but an effort to prolong Jesus' life in order to see if God the Father would send the prophet Elijah to rescue Him in accordance with Jewish tradition.

FULFILLMENT
John 19:28
After this, Jesus knowing that all things were now accomplished, that the Scripture might be fulfilled, saith, I thirst. **KJV**

22. Forsaken by God

PROPHECY DATE: 1000 - 300 B.C.
Psalm 22:1
My God, My God, why have you forsaken Me? **NKJV**

Some people take this verse to be a sign of desperation on our Lord's part in His final hour but nothing could be further from the truth. Jesus is not asking for an answer or an explanation for why He is suffering. He quotes from Psalm 22:1 which parallels the Suffering Servant theme of Isaiah chapter 53. He cried out to God because He was forsaken not because he was abandoned. He freely offered up His life for us, it was not taken from Him. When God looked down and saw our sins upon Christ who was our sinless substitute, He withdrew His presence from His Son. This separation crushed the Lord Jesus' heart as the filth of our sins caused Jesus momentary separation from God. Jesus became forsaken through suffering the punishment of death on the cross so that we may not be forsaken eternally come the final judgment.

FULFILLMENT
Matthew 27:46
And about the ninth hour Jesus cried with a loud voice, saying, Eli, Eli, lama sabachthani? that is to say, My God, my God, why hast thou forsaken me? **KJV**

23. Commit Himself to God

PROPHECY DATE: 1000 - 300 B.C.
Psalm 31:5
Into Your hand I commit my spirit. **NKJV**

When Jesus died on the cross He cried out, "It is finished." His work of redemption was complete once and for all. Jesus gave His own life on the cross and became the infinite and only sin offering that could make atonement for mankind's sins. God no longer requires the ongoing animal sacrifices from the hands of the high priests to make atonement for the people's sins. Christ's one sacrifice became sufficient, forever, never needing to be repeated. Jesus obtained our eternal redemption once for all time through the shedding of His own blood. There is no longer any need for an on-going sacrifice for those who have had their sins purged under God's New Covenant and whose names have been registered in heaven. Seeing the multitudes that would be saved by faith in the atoning blood of Christ satisfied God who would withhold His punishment from those who had been justified through faith.

FULFILLMENT
Luke 23:46
And when Jesus had cried out with a loud voice, He said, "Father, *'into Your hands I commit My spirit,'* " Having said this He breathed His last. **NKJV**

24. His Bones Would Remain Unbroken

PROPHECY DATE: 1000 - 300 B.C.
Psalm 34:20
He keepeth all his bones: not one of them is broken. **KJV**

Jesus would have suffered bone dislocation as the cross was lifted up with Him on it and then dropped down into its place in the ground. But in fulfilment of this prophecy not one of His bones was broken. This prophecy also parallels with the Passover lamb, which is a type of Christ, and was not to have any of its bones broken. While on the cross Jesus would have been in excruciating pain as He tried to breathe. The very word excruciating was invented to describe the agony of crucifixion. In order to exhale Jesus would have had to push down hard upon His nailed feet while pulling upon his wrists simultaneously through dislocated shoulders in order to lift up His body. This would have released stress from the diaphragm allowing Him to take a breath. Eventually Jesus died by asphyxiation but it was the weight of mankind's sins that would see Jesus breath his last.

FULFILLMENT
John 19:33
But when they came to Jesus, and saw that he was dead already, they broke not his legs. **KJV**

25. Darkness over the Land

PROPHECY DATE: 760 - 750 B.C.
Amos 8:9
And it shall come to pass in that day, saith the LORD GOD, that I will cause the sun to go down at noon, and I will darken the earth in the clear day. **KJV**

It was the third hour, 9 a.m. when Jesus was crucified. At the sixth hour which was noon the land was covered in darkness. At the ninth hour which was 3 p.m. Jesus gave up His spirit. The very same moment that Jesus died on the cross there was a lunar eclipse followed by a powerful earthquake that shook the entire land. These events were so fearful that the Roman centurion who was standing close by confessed on the spot that Jesus Christ was truly the Son of God. During all this chaos the veil in the temple was torn in two from top to bottom symbolising that ordinary people could now have direct access to the Holy of Holies, God Himself, through Christ's finished work at Calvary.

FULFILLMENT
Matthew 27:45
Now from the sixth hour there was darkness over all the land unto the ninth hour. **KJV**

26. His Side Would Be Pierced 27. His Heart Would Be Broken

PROPHECY DATE: About 500 B.C.
Zechariah 12:10
And I will pour upon the house of David, and upon the inhabitants of Jerusalem, the spirit of grace and of supplications: and they shall look upon me whom they have pierced, and they shall mourn for him, as one mourneth for *his* only *son*, and shall be in bitterness for him, as one that is in bitterness for *his* firstborn. **KJV**

There will be an out pouring of the Holy Spirit upon the nation of Israel during the last days. When this happens the Jews will come to the realization that they put to death their Messiah. They will look unto Him whom they pierced and bitterly mourn their loss. To be pierced literally means to have been thrust through. This is a reference to the spear used by the Roman soldier who pierced Jesus' heart to make sure He was dead. The large amount of blood loss experienced by Jesus on the day He was crucified would have increased His heart rate, resulting in heart failure. A gathering of fluid in the membrane around the heart and lungs was released when the Roman soldier entered his spear into Jesus side piercing His heart and lung. John describes blood and water coming from Jesus' side, exactly what modern medicine would expect to have happened, making John a credible eyewitness to the most important historic event ever.

FULFILLMENT
John 19:34
But one of the soldiers pierced His side with a spear, and immediately blood and water came out. **NKJV**

28. Buried in a Rich Mans Tomb

PROPHECY DATE: About 700 B.C.
Isaiah 53:9
And they made His grave with the wicked– But with the rich at His death, Because He had done no violence, Nor *was any* deceit in His mouth. **NKJV**

Men plotted a shameful burial place for Jesus after His crucifixion. But God assigned Jesus the tomb of Joseph of Arimathea among the rich as a reflection of Christ's innocence.

FULFILLMENT
Matthew 27:57 - 60
When the even was come, there came a rich man of Arimathaea, named Joseph, who also himself was Jesus' disciple: He went to Pilate, and begged the body of Jesus. Then Pilate commanded the body to be delivered. And when Joseph had

taken the body, he wrapped it in a clean linen cloth, And laid it in his own new tomb. **KJV**

29. *Rejected by His Own People*

PROPHECY DATE: About 700 B.C.
Isaiah 53:3
He is despised and rejected of men; a man of sorrows, and acquainted with grief: and we hid as it were *our* faces from him; he was despised, and we esteemed him not. **KJV**

Even Jesus' own brothers did not really believe that he was the Messiah. They had no desire to trust in Him or see Him glorified. None of the rulers of the Jewish nation believed in Him either. God had literally come to His own people of Israel in human form but they failed to recognise Him. Not only did the Pharisees not recognise Jesus as their Messiah but they prevented others from following Him. Just as it is today, many who are disinterested in the things of God will do almost everything in their power to prevent others, including members of their own family from becoming Christians.

FULFILLMENT
John 7:5, 48
For neither did his brethren believe in him. V 48; Have any of the rulers or of the Pharisees believed on him? **KJV**

CONCLUSION
It is statistically impossible that all these events would have converged randomly in the life of one person. It is not just a statistical impossibility that rules out the theory that Jesus engineered His prophecy fulfilments. There is no way in the world that Jesus could have manipulated the events and people throughout His life to respond in exactly the way necessary for it to appear that he was fulfilling all these predictions. The truth is that only God in human form could have lived His life in the person of Jesus Christ in order for these prophecies to have come to pass in the exact manner foretold. Any other explanation other than this being the supernatural work of God is just refusal to believe that God Himself is working out His eternal plan of redemption.

CHAPTER 5

Bible Prophecy and the Occult

Isaiah 42:9
Behold, the former things are come to pass, and new things do I declare: before they spring forth I tell you of them. **KJV**

Bible prophecy makes up one fourth of the written word of God and so it demands a serious study of the scriptures to understand this important area of inspired truth. Prophecy is based upon information that is received from God by men who were known as "prophets." Through their inspirational words prophets were described as God's servants, watchmen, holy men, and seers. These inspired messengers were chosen by God to declare His will by foretelling future events before they actually occurred. In the Torah, the first five books of the Old Testament, prophecy often consisted of a warning by God of the consequences should His people not hold fast to the Torah's instructions during the same time period as the prophet's life. Prophets also predicted great blessings for those who returned to behaviours and laws as written in the Torah, in obedience to God.

The Israelites were constantly warned against false prophet's who would seek to lead them away from their covenant relationship with God, into the sin of idolatry. They were to always test the prophets by their teachings, whether or not they led people to God or away from Him. If a prophet made a prediction that did not come to pass it was a sure sign that he had spoken presumptuously and no one needed to fear any curse he might pronounce. If a prophet preformed a miracle or made a prediction that came to pass, and then said, come let us follow other gods, he was not to be followed. The Law of Moses demanded that such a person be put to death by stoning because of his spiritual seduction. This law was extremely strict and acted as a deterrent to anyone who was not receiving their messages from God. Even if a close relative claimed to have received a vision or a dream from God and then enticed his family members to practice idolatry, he too would be put to death.

In the New Testament, prophecy is referred to as one of the spiritual gifts which is dispensed by the Holy Spirit to genuine believers. The purpose of any message from God is mainly to edify, exhort and comfort the members of the church or an individual believer in Jesus Christ and not just the individual exercising the gift. Since the bible is a complete work any prophet who claims to have additional truth from God is to be rejected. Although prophecy involves the predicting of future events, its main purpose is to communicate God's messages to the church, providing it with insight, warning, correction and encouragement. Unlike today's modern psychics God's prophets made prophecies that were 100% accurate every time.

The bible warns Christians to test the spirits. The Spirit of truth is the Holy Spirit who speaks through Godly prophets, words that are consistent with scripture. The spirit of error, literally counterfeit error or deception is of Satan and his angels who perform their work through false prophets and teachers. There are many false prophets and teachers in the church today that are very successful in their efforts to deceive people. We can test these false prophets and teachers to see if their messages are truly coming to us from the Lord. One way is to check and see if what they say matches up to what God has already said in the bible. Another way is to test their life-style, does it match up with the word of God? Do they always give to those who have need or are they always pronouncing blessings in exchange for money? What do they believe about Christ? Do they teach that Jesus is fully God and fully man? As Christians we need to weigh the words of anyone who claims to speak on behalf of God against what we know to be true in the bible. We are not to be so gullible that we confusingly accept the pronouncements of all and any prophet who claims to have a divine word from God.

Prophets were forbidden to have any contact with the dead or from conjuring up the deceased, an occult practice which is known as necromancy. This violation of God's law coincides with mediums, spiritists, fortune-tellers, séance leaders, astrologers and witchcraft, which God refers to as abominations. While millions read into their horoscopes every day or visit clairvoyants to seek spiritual foreknowledge or look to mediums to communicate with their deceased family members, the bible forbids such activities knowing the origin of these oracles of heathenism. Clairvoyants and mediums may seem like they have the hidden answers to all your questions but the real question that should be asked is, where are they getting their information from? One thing you can be sure of, it is not coming from God. In the book of Acts when Paul and Silas were going to a place of prayer, they met a slave girl who was possessed with a spirit of divination. This slave girl made plenty of money for her masters by fortune-telling and following Paul and Silas she would cry out; "These men are the servants of the Most High God, who proclaim to us the way of salvation," Acts 16:17 NKJV. But Paul became greatly annoyed and turning to the girl he commanded the unclean spirit to come out of her, and it did that very hour. Paul knew that the slave girl had spoken the truth concerning their ministry. Nevertheless, he was not going to give the familiar spirit (demon) in whom this girl was channelling the opportunity to distort the gospel's message after they had moved on.

So we can see that God is not the only one who uses forecasts of future events to gain people's attention, Satan does too, though with very limited accuracy. This is why participation in these occult practices should be avoided like the plague. People might be attracted to the occult with a desire to know about the future or perhaps superstition, loneliness or even dissatisfaction with traditional religious forms is the driving force behind ones curiosity with the supernatural. The tragedy is that people are being hoodwinked into communicating with supernatural evil forces, whereas what God offers us in His word is a chance to meet with the supernatural power of the Holy Spirit. Any interaction with the occult will not only lead a person away from God and his plan of redemption but can also cause oppression, fear, anxiety, and even possession when control over one's life is in the hands of the demonic. As we can see, playing around with the occult leads to serious repercussions, both psychologically and spiritually. To meet with our heavenly Father is much more exciting, satisfying and a whole lot wiser.

Many who have used the Ouija board are certain that they have been "enlightened" but Satan who transforms himself as an angel of light is the deceiver behind these subtle demonic gateways. Those without the Holy Spirit living in them are most vulnerable to the unholy deceptions of these spirit mediums who work off people's emotions and weak wills for an appropriate fee. They may even claim to be working on behalf of the Holy Spirit and disclose to you some truthful information concerning your personal life. But they are just as likely to give to you fabricated information on the whereabouts of a deceased family member you may be grieving. In biblical times any man or woman found to be a medium or who had a familiar spirit (demon) to aid them in their divination would have surely been put to death under God's law.

Sympathetic magic, which is an essential cornerstone to witchcraft, uses the process of divining the unnamed creative force to work favours. One who conjures spells by using this "dark force" is not receiving his empowerment from the Holy Spirit but rather from a very real demonic force. Wizards or male witches like the fictional character Harry Potter are actually collaborating with supernatural demonic agents and satanic forces to achieve their paranormal results. In Old Testament times wizards and witches would have also been put to death for their involvement in these occult practises. Unfortunately the prohibition of sorcery is just as much needed in our "tolerant" modern times as it was in Old Testament times thousands of years ago. Demons, Satanism and the occult are very real and dark sinister realities and are not games to be explored or dabbled in. Although Satan is not omnipresent, meaning he cannot be everywhere at once, he does have his own agents or demons that are at work in the unseen realms deceiving the minds of those who love not the truth found in God's word. One can therefore come to a better understanding of the consequences concerning their actions when they know what the bible has to say about all of these dangers.

Leviticus 19:31
'Give no regard to mediums and familiar spirits; do not seek after them, to be defiled by them: I *am* the LORD your God.' **NKJV**

Deuteronomy 18:10 - 12
There shall not be found among you *any one* that maketh his son or his daughter to pass through the fire, *or* that useth divination, *or* an observer of times, or an enchanter, or a witch. Or a charmer, or a consulter with familiar spirits, or a wizard, or a necromancer. For all that do these things *are* an abomination unto the LORD: and because of these abominations the LORD thy God doth drive them out from before thee. **KJV**

Isaiah 8:19 - 20
And when they say to you, "Seek those who are mediums and wizards, who whisper and mutter," should not a people seek their God? *Should they seek* the dead on behalf of the living? To the law and to the testimony! If they do not speak according to this word, *it is* because *there is* no light in them. **NKJV**

2 Corinthians 11:14 - 15
For Satan himself transforms himself into an angel of light. Therefore *it is* no great thing if his ministers also transform themselves into ministers of righteousness, whose end will be according to their works. **NKJV**

CHAPTER 6

End Time Prophecies

Isaiah 46:9 - 10
Remember the former things of old, For I *am* God, and *there is* no other; I *am* God, and *there is* none like Me, Declaring the end from the beginning, And from ancient times *things* that are not *yet* done. **NKJV**

One of my favourite TV programs during the mid to late 1990's was a serious called "Early Edition." It was about a guy called Gary Hobson played by actor Kyle Chandler, who was a stockbroker that got fired from his job and dumped by his wife. Gary lived in a hotel room in the busy city of Chicago Illinois in the U.S. where every morning at 6.30 a.m. he would wake up to the sound of his alarm clock followed by the crying of a ginger cat outside his front door. As he climbed out of bed to open the door the cat would come running in, mysteriously leaving behind at his doorstep a copy of the Chicago Sun-Times newspaper the day before it was actually published. Every day Gary would use his knowledge of tomorrow's headlines to prevent many terrible accidents from happening. But what if you were given a newspaper that allowed you to read about tomorrow's headlines before certain events took place. Think of the life changing experiences you would have and all the people that you could save. Knowing what disasters lay ahead would definitely have a serious impact on your life. More than that, what if this newspaper warned you about disasters that were going to directly affect you and your entire family? What if this newspaper could help save you and your loved ones from sudden destruction? You would certainly take the time to study every minute detail. What many people fail to realise is that the bible is filled with hundreds of end time prophecies and headline grabbing predictions.

From the very first book in the bible, Genesis, to the last book, Revelation, the bible is filled with over a thousand predictive prophecies. These prophecies are not vague or ambiguous in their predictions but very specific, very detailed and were made centuries in advance of their fulfilment. The bible contains prophecies about the rise and fall of kingdoms and nations plus many other prophecies concerning cities, individuals and events. Many of these predictions have already come to pass but there are still those which await future fulfilment. A large amount of Old Testament prophecies about the last days or end of the world, speak about the future of the Jews, the nation of Israel and the city of Jerusalem. A study of these Old Testament prophecies can reveal to us a detailed description surrounding the events which will take place in the Middle East and the rest of the world nearing the end of time. For example the bible foretold that there would come a day that the Jewish people would be scattered or dispersed all over the world, this has been fulfilled. The bible also predicted that whatever country the Jews would place their feet in, they would be persecuted, this has also happened. The bible foretold that after the Jews had been dispersed their land would become desolate, and it did. The bible also prophesied that in the last days prior to Christ's second coming God would gather His people, the Jews, from the four corners of the earth and plant them back in their ancestral homeland, and He has. The re-gathering of God's people is one of the most prolific prophecies to have come to pass and stands as a visible miracle that God is in control of mankind's destiny, especially the Jews. Knowledge of these prophecies should be producing converts worldwide but many people are still ignorant of these warning signs preceding Christ's second coming.

While historical events appear to happen by chance the bible reveals to us that history is unfolding according to God's precise plan which has been outlined thousands of years ago by His prophets. The re-establishment of Israel as an independent nation is probably one of the most important of all end time prophecies indicating Christ's soon return. For nearly two thousand years the land of Israel and its people were almost successfully crushed and a miracle was needed to revive them. That miracle was promised through many of God's prophets, centuries before it came to pass in May of 1948. In 1967 the Israelis captured the old city of Jerusalem during the Six-Day War and for the first time in almost two thousand years Jerusalem came under Israeli control. Given their long exile of over nineteen hundred years and the hostility of the occupants of Palestine toward them, any prediction of the Jews returning to their ancestral homeland was extremely unlikely. However, God foretold centuries in advance about the restoration of the Jews to their homeland and many who are alive today are witnesses to the fulfilment of this historical fact. In 1922 the League of Nations gave Great Britain the mandate over Palestine but Britain withdrew her mandate on the 14th May 1948 and the nation of Israel was born. There is no other nation in history who has managed so successfully to keep their national identity and language over hundreds of years, especially against the genocidal hatred repeatedly encountered by the Jews. The following prophecies provide further evidence that the bible is the inspired word of God. Since many of these prophecies are being fulfilled today we can be sure that we are living in the last days. In fact, the evidence of divine origin of the bible is becoming stronger as more and more of these ancient prophecies are being fulfilled.

1. Israel would be scattered into all Nations to Live in Fear and Persecution

God promised the people of Israel many great blessings if they would remain faithful to their covenant with Him. But if they did not remain faithful to their covenant they would be dispersed among the nations of the world. Unfortunately, after the rejection of their Messiah Jesus Christ, Israel's sins led them into exile from the Promised Land for nearly two millennia. In A.D. 70 the Roman forces led by Titus attacked and destroyed the city of Jerusalem and its Holy Temple. More than one million Jews were murdered and hundreds of thousands were forced into exile and slavery. In A.D. 135 The Roman Emperor Hadrian changed the name of Judea to Syria Palestina "Palestine" after Israel's ancient enemies the Philistines, in an attempt to banish Jewish connection from the land. This began the dispersion or Diaspora of the Jewish people from one end of the earth to the other. Scattered abroad into every nation the Jews have been reviled, abused and persecuted everywhere they have gone. God decreed no comfort for them and Anti-Semitism became their way of life throughout history.

In A.D. 1095 Pope Urban II (1042-99) launched the first Crusade to retake Jerusalem from the Muslims who had controlled it since A.D. 638. Urban preached a sermon in Clermont France proclaiming that the Turks and Arabs had conquered their territories. "I or rather, the Lord begs you," he stated, "to destroy that vile race from the land." A pilgrimage believed to weigh heavy toward ones salvation was led to the Holy Land which turned into a war against "the infidels" or unbelievers. Pope Urban decreed that all heretics were to be tortured and killed promising "Christians" who took part in the bloody crusade a full pardon from their sins. In A.D. 1099 Jerusalem fell to the royal Crusaders. On taking Jerusalem for the "Holy Mother Church" Muslim blood flowed ankle-deep on the Temple Mount. Infants were thrown against walls and Jews were rounded up like cattle into the synagogue and burned alive. The Jews also suffered massacre and expulsion from various countries during the Crusades. They were even used as scapegoats for the spreading of the plague known as the Black Death or bubonic plague and were blamed for the poisoning of wells during the 14th century. As a result many Jews were slaughtered. In A.D. 1478 Pope Sixtus IV (1414-84) issued a papal bull allowing for the creation of the Spanish Inquisition. For centuries after many Jews were imprisoned, tortured and burned alive.

In May of 1939 the S.S. St Louis ocean liner carried 937 Jewish men women and children refugees from nazi persecution to Cuba. But anti-Jewish hate caused the Cuban government under Federico Laredo Brú to refuse passengers asylum, even though they carried valid visas on entry into Havana harbour. In fear of returning to Germany Captain Schroeder set course for the U.S. and a telegram was sent to President Roosevelt. But no reply was to be received. In fact, the State Department sent word that it would not interfere in Cuban affairs and also refused passengers asylum even though many carried valid papers. The fleeing refugees had no choice but to return to Europe where many found themselves back under nazi rule. Eventually many of those who had returned to Europe faced death in Hitler's gas ovens. The murder of over six million Jews in Hitler's extermination camps during World War II was not just an isolated event but part of an ongoing Anti-Semitic epidemic. During their dispersion the Jewish people found no resting place for the soles of their feet earning them the name of wandering Jews. But God providentially preserved them as a separate people during their worldwide wanderings. One only has to look up the word "Jews" in any encyclopedia for a detailed history concerning the endless list of persecutors who have committed despicable crimes against God's chosen people. This particular prophecy appears many times throughout the Old Testament and has literally been fulfilled in one ethnic group.

Leviticus 26:33
And I will scatter you among the heathen, and will draw out a sword after you: and your land shall be desolate, and your cities waste. **KJV**

Deuteronomy 28:37, 63, 64, 65
"And you shall become an astonishment, a proverb, and a byword among all nations where the LORD will drive you." V 63; "And you shall be plucked from off the land which you go to possess." V 64; "Then the LORD will scatter you among all peoples, from one end of the earth to the other." V 65; "And among those nations you shall find no rest, nor shall the sole of your foot have a resting place; but there the LORD will give you a trembling heart, failing eyes, and anguish of soul." **NKJV**

Jeremiah 29:18
And I will persecute them with the sword, with the famine, and with the pestilence, and will deliver them to be removed to all the kingdoms of the earth, to be a curse, and an astonishment, and a hissing, and a reproach, among all the nations whither I have driven them. **KJV**

Luke 21:24
And they shall fall by the edge of the sword, and shall be led away captive into all nations: and Jerusalem shall be trodden down of the Gentiles, until the times of the Gentiles be fulfilled. **KJV**

2. The Rebirth of Israel and the Regathering of the Jews

The rebirth of Israel as an independent nation is one of the most significant of all end time prophecies. No other nation in history has ever ceased to exist for nearly two thousand years and then return to take centre stage in world affairs. Despite the Jews' hardship God promised that they would not be exiled forever nor would they be assimilated into the land of their enemies. God would fulfil His promise and gather His people from all the worldly nations to which they had been scattered and restore them back to their homeland. The prophet Isaiah predicted the physical restoration of Israel with these words: "Who has heard such a thing? Who has seen such things? Shall the earth be made to give birth in one day? *Or* shall a nation be born at once? For as soon as Zion was in labour, She gave birth to her children," Isaiah 66:8 NKJV. The fig tree considered a symbol of prosperity was used by the Lord Jesus in Matthew's gospel chapter 24:32 - 35, to describe the future restoration of Israel. The budding of the fig tree not only speaks of the emergence of Israel as a nation, it also indicates the fact that we are moving closer to Christ's return, which in itself will bring about Israel's full spiritual restoration.

On the 29th November 1947 the General Assembly of the United Nations adopted a Resolution calling for the establishment of an independent Jewish State. Then on May 14th 1948 the British withdrew their mandate and the nation of Israel was literally "born in a day." Against overwhelming odds Israel declared her sovereign independence for the first time since the Babylonian takeover in 606 B.C. The very next day the British pulled out ending British control of the land and the United States among other nations issued statements recognizing Israel's sovereignty. The Jewish people have since returned to their homeland from Europe, Russia, Ethiopia, Asia, and the U.S. with a population expected to reach 8.5 million by the year 2020. The rebirth of Israel is an event which is unprecedented in the history of mankind. No other ancient nation has maintained its heritage and identity after centuries of exile. For hundreds of years men have criticised the prophecies concerning the restoration of Israel. Yet Israel's existence today and the re-gathering of the Jews from all parts of the world stands as irrefutable proof that the bible is the true and inspired word of the living God.

Genesis 13:15
"For all the land which you see I give to you and your descendants forever."
NKJV

Isaiah 43:5 - 6
"Fear not, for I *am* with you; I will bring your descendants from the east, And gather you from the west; I will say to the north, 'Give them up!' And to the south, 'Do not keep them back!' Bring My sons from afar, And my daughters from the ends of the earth." NKJV

Jeremiah 31:7 - 8
For thus says the LORD: "Sing with gladness for Jacob, And shout among the chief of the nations; Proclaim, give praise, and say, 'O LORD, save Your people, The remnant of Israel!' Behold, I will bring them from the north country, And gather them from the ends of the earth." NKJV

Ezekiel 36:24
For I will take you from among the heathen, and gather you out of all countries, and will bring you into your own land. KJV

Amos 9:15
"I will plant them in their land, And no longer shall they be pulled up From the land I have given them," Says the LORD your God. NKJV

Zephaniah 3:20
"At that time I will bring you back, Even at the time I gather you; For I will give you fame and praise Among all the peoples of the earth, When I return your captives before your eyes," Says the LORD. NKJV

Matthew 24:32 - 33
"Now learn this parable from the fig tree: When its branch has already become tender and puts forth leaves, you know that summer *is* near. So you also, when you see all these things, know that it is near–at the doors!" NKJV

3. *Israel Shall Blossom and Bud*

The prophet Isaiah predicted that in the last days Israel would blossom and bud and fill the face of the earth with fruit. Since the return of the Jewish exiles to their homeland, Israel has been restored to the original conditions of her ancient past as a land flowing with milk and honey. Once described as a wilderness, today Israel's agriculture is thriving. With an increase in rainfall plus Israel's irrigation technology, the once desolate land has been cultivated into one of the most fertile countries in the world. Today there are two hundred and fifty million trees covering two hundred and fifty thousand acres which have transformed the complete environment of the Promised Land into a lush modern day Eden. Israel produces most of its own food but also exports millions of euro worth of flowers, seeds, fruit, and ornamental plants. The returning Jews have transformed the once desolate land of Israel into one of the most agriculturally efficient lands on earth thus fulfilling Isaiah's prophecy.

Isaiah 27:6
Israel shall blossom and bud, and fill the face of the world with fruit. **KJV**

Isaiah 35:7
And the parched ground shall become a pool, and the thirsty land springs of water. **KJV**

Ezekiel 36:34 - 36
"The desolate land shall be tilled instead of lying desolate in the sight of all who pass by. So they will say, 'This land that was desolate has become like the garden of Eden; and the wasted, desolate, and ruined cities *are now* fortified *and* inhabited.' Then the nations which are left all around you shall know that I, the LORD, have rebuilt the ruined places *and* planted what was desolate. I, the LORD, have spoken *it*, and I will do *it*." **NKJV**

4. *Jerusalem a Cup of Trembling*

About 2,500 years ago the prophet Zechariah foretold that in the last days Jerusalem would become a cup of trembling and a burdensome stone to all nations. This prophecy was written at a time when Jerusalem lay in ruins and its history thereafter has been of repeated destruction. However, today Jerusalem stands at the centre of world affairs with more resolutions passed by the UN Security Council on the status and destiny of Jerusalem than on any other city in the world. Many of the ancient Muslim nations that surround Israel occupy land which is five hundred times larger than Israel but still they persist in the annihilation of the Jews and possession of their land. Because the Arab nations refuse to accept a Jewish state, resistance has become strong with the formation of many Islamic terrorist organizations. Incitement to hatred of the Jews and Israel is sponsored by the Palestinian Authority. Text books in PA school systems from elementary through high school are filled with anti Semitic expressions against the Jews. Sixth graders read of a young boy growing up with a love for Jihad (holy war) flowing through his veins and filling every fibre of his being. Joy comes only at the sight of the enemy lying dead. Jihad and martyrdom consume children's poems with fifth graders memorizing such lines as, "I shall take my soul in my hand and hurl it into the abyss of death." Suicide bombers have become role models for Palestinian children as 70% of children from the Gaza strip express hopes of martyrdom. Hezbollah, a Shi'a terrorist organization, backed by Iran also resists Israeli occupation calling for her destruction. In October 2005 the Iranian president Mahmoud Ahmadinejad made a disturbing statement, that Israel should be wiped off the map and added that the Holocaust was nothing more than a myth. The call for Israel's destruction is commonplace in the Middle East. This can be seen and heard of every day, on Hezbollah TV, in Syrian media, and in Egyptian editorials appearing in semi-official newspapers. Israel is completely surrounded by Muslim nations that will not rest until the very existence of Israel has been eliminated. According to the bible the threat of war in the Middle East will grow until it threatens the peace of the entire world. There may be periods of relative peace concerning Jerusalem in the coming future but it will not last. The bible predicts that the surrounding nations will gather against Israel in the final days for what is known as the battle of Armageddon. But God will ultimately destroy all the nations which will come against Israel and His Holy City Jerusalem in the last days.

Psalm 83:3 - 4
They have taken crafty counsel against thy people, and consulted against thy hidden ones. They have said, Come, and let us cut them off from *being* a nation; that the name of Israel may be no more in remembrance. **KJV**

Zechariah 12:2 - 3, 9
Behold, I will make Jerusalem a cup of trembling unto all the people round about, when they shall be in the siege both against Judah *and* against Jerusalem. And in that day will I make Jerusalem a burdensome stone for all people: all that burden themselves with it shall be cut in pieces, though all the people of the earth be gathered together against it. V 9; And it shall come to pass in that day, *that* I will seek to destroy all the nations that come against Jerusalem. **KJV**

Revelation 16:16
And he gathered them together into a place called in the Hebrew tongue Armageddon. **KJV**

5. Man would be Capable of destroying all Life on Earth

Jesus foretold that in the last days man would be capable of destroying all life on planet earth. At the time Jesus made this prophecy wars were being fought on horseback with swords and spears. But today with the widespread advancements in global technology the world holds enough devastating nuclear, biological and chemical weapons to destroy every human being on the planet. The prophet Zechariah gives to us a graphical description of how Israel's enemies will be destroyed during earth's final battle, Armageddon; And this shall be the plague with which the LORD will strike all the people who fought against Jerusalem: Their flesh shall dissolve while they stand on their feet, Their eyes shall dissolve in their sockets, And their tongues shall dissolve in their mouths, Zechariah 14:12 NKJV. This verse of scripture describes the exact effects of nuclear weapons as used by the U.S. during the Second World War. When America dropped its atomic bombs on Hiroshima and Nagasaki in Japan the explosion literally vaporised people before they could move a muscle. The results were absolutely devastating with a combined death toll reaching well over 120,000 people. It is no secret that Israel posses nuclear weapons and they are very much prepared to use them if they are attacked. With tensions constantly growing in the Middle East the reality of a nuclear exchange seems imminent. It is estimated that Iran has produced enough enriched uranium to manufacture a nuclear arsenal. The Iranian president Mahmoud Ahmadinejad, a Shi'a Islamic Fundamentalist, would actually relish a clash with Israel. He believes that Israel's destruction would somehow bring upon the global spread of Islam, ushering in the arrival of Islam's expected messianic-like figure Al-Mahdi, who will bring bloodshed to all infidels.

Matthew 24:21 - 22
"For then there will be great tribulation, such as has not been since the beginning of the world until this time, no, nor ever shall be. And unless those days were shortened, no flesh would be saved; but for the elect's sake those days will be shortened." **NKJV**

2 Peter 3:10
But the day of the Lord will come as a thief in the night; in which the heavens shall pass away with a great noise, and the elements shall melt with fervent heat, the earth also and the works that are therein shall be burned up. **KJV**

6. The Water of the Euphrates River Dried Up

In the book of Revelation the apostle John foretold of a time when the great river Euphrates would be dried up in preparation for the final battle of Armageddon. This would allow the enormous army of 200 million soldiers prophesied by John to march from Asia toward northern Israel for an invasion. This prophecy could only be fulfilled if there was a natural disaster or if a great deal of manual labour was to take place allowing this army passage to invade Israel. Amazingly during the 1980's and 1990's construction work began on a serious of dams which stretch along the Tigris and Euphrates rivers. The Ataturk Dam located in the South Eastern Anatolia Region of Turkey was one of the many dams which was constructed and completed in this project. It is also one of the largest rock filled dams in the world standing at nearly six hundred feet high and six thousand feet long. For the first time in history the headwaters of the great river Euphrates can be dried up exactly as foretold by the apostle John. The Euphrates River has been for thousands of years the dividing line between the Middle East and China and the Far East. But today it is no longer an impenetrable barrier between the armies of the east and the west.

Revelation 9:14 - 16
Saying to the sixth angel which had the trumpet, Loose the four angels which are bound in the great river Euphrates. And the four angels were loosed, which were prepared for an hour, and a day, and a month, and a year, for to slay the third part of men. And the number of the army of the horsemen *were* two hundred thousand thousand: and I heard the number of them. **KJV**

Revelation 16:12
And the sixth angel poured out his vial upon the great river Euphrates; and the water thereof was dried up, that the way of the kings of the east might be prepared. **KJV**

7. The East Gate Sealed until Christ's Second Coming

The Eastern Gate or Golden Gate as it is referred to in Christian literature is one of eight gates built into the walls surrounding the Temple Mount in Jerusalem. It is located on the eastern side of the Temple Mount opposite the Mount of Olives and provides the only entrance into the courtyards from the Kidron Valley to the East. The Gate was destroyed when the Romans sacked the Temple in A.D. 70 thus fulfilling Jesus' prophecy that; "There shall not be left here one stone upon another, that shall not be thrown down," Matthew 24:2 KJV. In A.D. 1541 the

Gate was sealed up by Muslim conquerors, the Ottoman Turks. Legend suggests that Suleiman the Magnificent, the Ottoman Sultan, learned from Jewish rabbis that the Messiah, whom they described as a great military leader would be sent by God from the east and would enter through the Eastern Gate. To stop this from happening during Suleiman's reign the Sultan had the Gate sealed up thinking that it would prevent the Messiah's coming. The Muslims also planted a cemetery in front of the Gate believing that no holy man would defile himself by walking through a Muslim cemetery. These efforts though to stop the Messiah from entering from the way of the east, were done so in vain because the Lord Jesus Christ had already presented Himself as the promised Messiah long before the Ottoman Turks sealed up the Gates entrance. During the last week of His ministry Jesus of Nazareth rode a donkey from the Mount of Olives down into the Kidron Valley and up to the Eastern Gate. There He entered into the Temple, not inside the sanctuary but into the Temple courts. The valley was filled with thousands of admirers waving palm branches and chanting; "Hosanna to the Son of David," Matthew 21:9 KJV. According to the prophet Ezekiel the Eastern Gate would remain sealed until the Messiah returns. Today, just as Ezekiel had foretold the Eastern Gate remains sealed off and will do so until Christ's second coming. This landmark remains as visible evidence of fulfilled prophecy and stands as undeniable evidence to sceptics worldwide as to the divine nature of the bible. Unfortunately many people look upon the sealed Gate as merely a coincidence, but they will realise their folly when Jesus Christ returns to enter the Eastern Gate once again.

Ezekiel 43:1 - 2, 4
Afterward he brought me to the gate, *even* the gate that looketh toward the east: And, behold, the glory of the God of Israel came from the way of the east: and his voice *was* like a noise of many waters: and the earth shined with his glory. V 4; And the glory of the LORD came into the house by the way of the gate whose prospect *is* toward the east. **KJV**

Ezekiel 44:1 - 3
Then he brought me back the way of the gate of the outward sanctuary which looketh toward the east; and it *was* shut. Then said the LORD unto me; This gate shall be shut, it shall not be opened, and no man shall enter in by it; because the LORD, the God of Israel, hath entered in by it, therefore it shall be shut. *It is* for the prince; the prince, he shall sit in it to eat bread before the LORD; he shall enter by the way of the porch of *that* gate, and shall go out by the way of the same. **KJV**

8. The Rebuilding of the Third Temple in Jerusalem

One of the most interesting of all end time prophecies to be fulfilled is the re-building of the Third Temple on the Temple Mount in Jerusalem. The first Temple was built by King Solomon but was destroyed by the Babylonians in 586 B.C. The second Temple was built in 536 B.C. but was later destroyed by the Romans in A.D. 70. After the Jews recaptured the Temple Mount from Arab control during the Six - Day War in 1967 the stage was set for the rebuilding of the Third Temple. But in an effort to help diffuse tensions between the Arabs and Jews, Israel permitted the Muslims control over the structures on the Temple Mount. This restricted Jewish access to the Temple Mount making the prospects of construction on a Third Temple seem almost bleak. The Temple Mount is known by Muslims as the Nobel Sanctuary and is home to both the Al-Aqsa Mosque and the Dome of the Rock, an Islamic shrine which is located at the centre of the Temple Mount. This Islamic shrine is believed to be covering the site where the Muslim's prophet Muhammad ascended into heaven. It is also believed to be the site of the two previous Jewish Temples. If this Islamic shrine is indeed built upon the foundation of the First and Second Temple site then construction on a future Third Temple would seem virtually impossible. However, there is dispute among Jewish archaeologists as to the original site of Solomon's Temple. Some archaeologists suggest that a Third Temple could indeed be built in the open area directly north to the Dome of the Rock. According to the Prophet Ezekiel, when the Messiah returns He will enter the Third Temple through the now sealed Eastern Gate. If the Third Temple was built to the north of the Dome of the Rock then entrance through the now sealed Eastern Gate would lead directly into the new Temple just as Ezekiel predicted. In the book of Revelation the apostle John was told by an angel to rise and measure the Temple of God and the altar but told to leave out the court which is outside the Temple because it has been given to the Gentiles, meaning non Jewish. This prophecy indicates that both the Dome of the Rock and the Third Holy Temple could co-exist on the Temple Mount during the last days. Preparations are already under way as the Temple Institute which is based in the Old City of Jerusalem has in its possession many of the needed sacred vessels, utensils and priestly garments that will be needed for Temple worship and sacrifice. There are also hundreds of young Jew-ish men training for the Levitical priesthood for the re-establishment of ancient Temple sacrifices. The bible also indicates that a red heifer without blemish must be born and sacrificed to produce the waters of purification in order to cleanse the Temple objects, the priests and the Temple Mount from spiritual defilement. The Temple Institute is at present actively seeking to acquire a kosher red heifer which meets the qualifications described in the book of Numbers chapter 19:2 - 9. These and many other developments may indeed prepare the way for the Israeli Jewish authorities to begin planning for a future Third Temple just as the ancient prophets foretold.

Isaiah 2:2
And it shall come to pass in the last days, *that* the mountain of the LORD'S house shall be established in the top of the mountains, and shall be exalted above the hills; and all nations shall flow unto it. **KJV**

Amos 9:11
"On that day I will raise up The tabernacle of David, which has fallen down, And repair its damages; I will raise up its ruins, And rebuild it as in the days of old." **NKJV**

Haggai 2:9
The glory of this latter house shall be greater than of the former, saith the LORD of hosts: and in this place will I give peace, saith the LORD of hosts. **KJV**

Revelation 11:1 - 2
Then I was given a reed like a measuring rod. And the angel stood, saying, "Rise and measure the temple of God, the altar, and those who worship there. But leave out the court which is outside the temple, and do not measure it, for it has been given to the Gentiles. And they will tread the holy city underfoot *for* forty-two months." **NKJV**

9. The Revived Roman Empire

About 2,500 years ago the prophet Daniel received a vision from God of four strange beasts representing the four world empires which are now history. The first beast, a lion, is believed to have represented the Babylonian Empire which was ruled under king Nebuchadnezzar. The second beast, a bear, represented the Medo-Persian Empire. The third beast, a leopard, represented the Macedonian Empire under Alexander the Great and the fourth beast represented the Roman Empire. The fourth beast is described differently from all the beasts that were before it. It was exceedingly strong and terrifying, having huge iron teeth which devoured the known world breaking and trampling all who opposed it. The iron teeth speak of Rome's unmatched military strength and the trampling illustrates the burden of Rome's culture and laws on conquered nations. According to the prophet Daniel there would be a future revival of the Roman Empire or fourth beast in the last days in a more powerful form to control the earth before Christ's return. The beast is described as having ten horns, a term that depicts power or authority and is believed to be a confederation of ten kings or world leaders who will rule in the area of the old Roman Empire during the last days. From these ten horns three would be replaced by another horn, small with eyes like the eyes of a man. The eyes of this little horn are a sign of supernatural intelligence which clearly embodies the Antichrist.

The EU is definitely becoming a world power with striking similarities to the fourth kingdom or fourth beast of Daniel's prophecy. The signs for the fulfilment of this prophecy began in 1957 when six European nations gathered together to sign the Treaty of Rome establishing the European Economic Community (EEC). This treaty brought six major European nations together for the first time in history since the days of the Roman Empire. In 1965 the Brussels Treaty was signed bringing about the process of rebuilding the old Roman Empire through the reunification of European nations under one political and economic system. The modern day unification of Europe, the European Union (EU) is an economic and political union of 27 member states which were established by the Treaty of Maastricht on 1 November 1993. From a political and economic stand point it may soon be the largest economy in the world and the most powerful political entity on earth, which looks to be setting the platform for the Roman Empire in its final form. The EU has already succeeded in implementing a common European parliament, court, currency and a strong military. Once a nation becomes a member of the EU and surrenders its sovereign powers to the Executive Commission of the European Union there will be no easy exit. A world power representing so many nations and ethnic groups could easily become a very influential leader at the United Nations. From this revived Roman Empire the world will soon see the rise of a global dictator who will begin to fulfil his role as the Antichrist. The bible says through false peace he will deceive many and will fulfil his ambition to dominate the world. Perhaps the Antichrist will appear to have solved the Middle East conflict through the creation of a Palestinian state. This may even bring about the rebuilding of the Third Temple on the Temple Mount in Jerusalem. The Antichrist will also fulfil yet another prophecy by entering the rebuilt Temple, where we are told he will set himself up as God and demand to be worshipped as God. But the Antichrist's physical body will ultimately be destroyed by the second coming of Christ, and his spirit, along with all those who worship him, will be cast into hell forever.

Daniel 7:7 - 8, 23 - 25

"After this I saw in the night visions, and behold, a forth beast, dreadful and terrible, exceedingly strong. It had huge iron teeth; it was devouring, breaking in pieces, and trampling the residue with its feet. It *was* different from all the beasts that *were* before it, and it had ten horns. I was considering the horns, and there was another horn, a little one, coming up among them, before whom three of the first horns were plucked out by the roots. And there, in this horn, *were* eyes like the eyes of a man, and mouth speaking pompous words." V 23 - 25; Thus he said: The forth beast shall be A forth kingdom on earth, Which shall be different from all *other* kingdoms, And shall devour the whole earth, Trample it and break it in pieces. The ten horns *are* ten kings *Who* shall arise from this kingdom. And another shall rise after them; He shall be different from the first *ones*, And shall subdue three kings. He shall speak *pompous* words against the Most High, Shall persecute the saints of the Most High, And shall intend to change times and law. **NKJV**

2 Thessalonians 2:3 - 4, 8 - 10

Let no one deceive you by any means; for *that Day will not come* unless the falling away comes first, and the man of sin is revealed, the son of perdition, who opposes and exalts himself above all that is called God or that is worshiped, so that he sits as God in the temple of God, showing himself that he is God. V 8 - 10; And then the lawless one will be revealed, whom the Lord will consume with the breath of his mouth and destroy with the brightness of His coming. The coming of the *lawless one* is according to the working of Satan, with all power, signs, and lying wonders, and with all unrighteous deception among those who perish, because they did not receive the love of the truth, that they might be saved. **NKJV**

10. *The Mark of the Beast 666*

In the book of Revelation the apostle John describes a time when no human being on the planet will be able to buy or sell without the Mark of the Beast. This mark is to be received in the forehead, perhaps a scanning of the iris, or in the right hand. The bible tells us that no one will be able to survive economically without this mark. The world is already moving toward a cashless society and with today's global technology and the increase use of biometrics, an identification computer chip the size of a grain of rice could simply be planted under the skin to allow all trading. This chip could hold an encyclopedia's worth of information concerning any individual on the planet, including their medical and financial records. A cashless society will virtually remove all crime such as abductions, muggings, drug trafficking, terrorism and tax evasion as purchases would only be made possible by electronic transfer. This security proof idea may seem to appear wonderful news to the whole world but it could also be used by the coming Antichrist for a much sinister purpose. According to the book of Revelation anyone who receives the Mark of the Beast from this global dictator, known as Antichrist, will ultimately be cast into the lake of fire which the bible describes as the second death. The computer technology is already available for everyone to receive this mark on a global level and once the chip has been implanted it will be impossible to avoid detection. With an identification chip planted underneath the flesh this could indeed be the vehicle through which the Mark of the Beast 666 will be distributed. The apostle John could not have imagined how the future could hold such incredible cashless technology unless God revealed this information to him through divine revelation.

Revelation 13:16 - 18
And he causeth all, both small and great, rich and poor, free and bond, to receive a mark in their right hand, or in their foreheads: And that no man might buy or sell, save he that had the mark, or the name of the beast, or the number of his name. Here is wisdom. Let him that hath understanding count the number of the beast: for it is the number of a man; and his number *is* Six hundred threescore *and* six. **KJV**

Revelation 14:11
And the smoke of their torment ascendeth up forever and ever: and they have no rest day nor night, who worship the beast and his image, and whosoever receiveth the mark of his name. **KJV**

Revelation 21:8
But the fearful, and unbelieving, and the abominable, and murderers, and whoremongers, and sorcerers, and idolaters, and all liars, shall have their part in the lake which burneth with fire and brimstone: which is the second death. **KJV**

11. The World to Witness Events Simultaneously

The bible foretells that in the last days God will send two witnesses into Jerusalem to proclaim the gospel of Jesus Christ for three and a half years during the Tribulation. But these two witnesses will be slain and their bodies will remain on the streets of Jerusalem for three and a half days without being permitted burial in a tomb. During this time we are told that the whole world will see their dead bodies and the people of the earth will celebrate and send gifts to each other in response to the deaths of both these prophets. The only way this prophecy could be fulfilled is through the invention of television and the deployment of global satellite communication networks. This would allow every person on the planet to see the bodies of God's two prophets laid out on the streets of Jerusalem as prophesied by the apostle John, images that we are already familiar with today. When the apostle John wrote the book of Revelation in A.D. 90 it would have been absolutely impossible for him to have known exactly how this prophecy might be fulfilled. The promise is however that this future event will come to pass.

Revelation 11:9 - 10
Then *those* from the peoples, tribes, tongues, and nations will see their dead bodies three-and-a-half days, and not allow their dead bodies to be put into graves. And those who dwell on the earth will rejoice over them, make merry, and send gifts to one another, because these two prophets tormented those who dwell on the earth. **NKJV**

12. The Gospel would be preached to the Whole World

When Jesus was in the house of Simon the leper, a woman came to Him with an expensive flask of fragrant oil and began to pour it on His Head whilst he sat at the table. When Jesus' disciples saw this they were displeased and said, this oil could have been sold for a lot and the money given to the poor. But having overheard His disciples, Jesus said to them, why are you troubling this women, can't you see that she has done a good work for Me? There will always be poor people among you, but as for Me, you will not always have. In pouring this oil on My body she has anointed Me for My burial. I tell you the truth, wherever this gospel is preached in the whole world, what this woman has done for Me will also be spoken of as a memorial to her.

Today, portions or the entire bible have been translated into well over two thousand different languages making the bible the most translated book in history. Over 90% of the world's population have already heard the gospel through TV, radio, the internet and missionaries. The gospel or good news of salvation has also been preached in every age of history throughout the entire world. And just as Jesus foretold, the story concerning the woman's good act of service has been immortalised through the ministering of the gospel. Only the Son of God could have known that the gospel concerning His own death, burial and resurrection was going to be preached in every nation throughout the entire world before He was even crucified.

Matthew 24:14
And this gospel of the kingdom shall be preached in all the world for a witness unto all nations; and then shall the end come. **KJV**

Matthew 26:13
"Assuredly, I say to you, wherever this gospel is preached in the whole world, what this woman has done will also be told as a memorial to her." **NKJV**

Luke 21:33
Heaven and earth shall pass away: but my words shall not pass away. **KJV**

Revelation 14:6
And I saw another angel fly in the midst of heaven, having the everlasting gospel to preach unto them that dwell on the earth, and to every nation, and kindred, and tongue, and people. **KJV**

13. There Would be an Increase in False Christ's, Wars, Famines, Pestilences and Earthquakes during the Last Days

As Jesus was sitting on the Mount of Olives His disciples came to Him and asked, what would be the signs that will accumulate nearing His second coming and the end of the world? Jesus warned them saying many would come in His name claiming to be the Christ. There would be wars and rumours of wars. Nation would rise against nation and kingdom against kingdom. There would be famines, diseases and earthquakes in various places. All these are the beginning of sorrows. Today we are seeing the fulfilment of these warning signs as never before. The world is literally flooded with cults and false religions each promoting their very own man-made version of "Jesus Christ," with the New Age Movement and Eastern religions at the top of the list. This century has also seen more people killed through warfare than in any other period in history. There are at least 40 to 50 major armed conflicts going on in the world a present. Famine is also a constant finding in third world countries such as Africa, Asia, and Latin America. During the 20th century an estimated 70 million people died as a result of famine and today almost a billion people living under the poverty line are dying of starvation. Disease which the bible refers to as pestilence has always been common but according to the bible during the last days there will be a significant increase in new and deadly infectious diseases that will claim the lives of millions. AIDS, said to be world's fastest spreading epidemic is responsible for claiming the lives of over twenty five million people. Other innumerable diseases such as Ebola, SARS, bird flu, polio, and the latest strain of Swine Flu are growing at an alarming rate. Despite medical advances we are also seeing the rise of old diseases such as cholera, malaria and tuberculosis. TB claims the lives of three million people every year. The number and intensity of earthquakes in this century alone has also been higher than any other time in history. Seismologists, who study earthquakes and their phenomena, are witnessing some of the most destructive geophysical forces ever recorded. The bible says as a woman's birth pangs increase in frequency and strength nearing the time of her delivery, so too will the planet earth groan in labour pangs drawing nearer to Christ's return. Many of these conditions have already existed to a certain extent throughout history. But together all these signs are to continue in intensity and severity prior to Christ's second coming just as Jesus had foretold.

Matthew 24:3 - 8
And as he sat upon the mount of Olives, the disciples came unto him privately, saying, Tell us, when shall these things be? and what *shall be* the sign of thy coming, and of the end of the world? And Jesus answered and said unto them, Take heed that no man deceive you. For many shall come in my name, saying, I am Christ; and shall deceive many. And ye shall hear of wars and rumours of wars: see that ye be not troubled: for all *these things* must come to pass, but the end is not yet. For nation shall rise against nation, and kingdom against kingdom: and there shall be famines, and pestilences, and earthquakes, in divers places. All these *are* the beginning of sorrows. **KJV**

Romans 8:21 - 22
Because the creation itself also will be delivered from the bondage of corruption into the glorious liberty of the children of God. For we know that the whole creation groans and labors with birth pangs together until now. **NKJV**

14. Moral Decline and Blasphemy

The apostle Paul foretold that in the last days the world would become an increasingly wicked and violent place. Men would be lovers of money and pleasure rather than lovers of God. Jesus taught that in last days immediately preceding his second coming that the condition of the world would be similar to the days of Noah. For in Noah's day the earth was filled with corruption and violence and the wickedness of man had become increasingly great. The lusts of the flesh had become the driving force behind the rejection of God and sexual immorality was widespread. God was grieved in His heart and sorry that he had made man because man's wickedness was great and the thoughts of his heart were continually evil all the time. But Noah, being a righteous man found favour in the eyes of God. Noah along with his wife, three sons and their wives were saved from

God's judgment by entering the ark before God flooded the entire earth. Jesus also spoke of Lot, when he, his wife and daughters left Sodom. It rained fire and brimstone from heaven destroying the wicked city. The signs relating to Sodom's destruction bear a striking similarity to those of Noah's day. They ate, drank, they bought and sold, they planted, they built but God was absent from their lives. They were busybodies, gossipmongers and had become sexually perverse. When God sent two angels to warn Lot of the coming destruction, the men of Sodom surrounded his home demanding God's visitors to come out so they could rape them. The moral condition surrounding these two events, the global flood of Noah's day and the destruction of Sodom and Gomorrah are but a shadow of the coming judgment upon the earth prior to Christ's second coming.

In today's world the pursuit of self-gratification, fame and riches, rather than the pursuit of purpose, meaning and God is leading many down the same wide path of destruction. God's clear warning signs are being phased out by the liberal secular humanist agenda that says to us, if it feels good do it. Television screens have become polluted with every heinous sin imaginable in some of the sickest movies ever made. Our children are constantly being bombarded by scenes of murder, rape, sexual immorality, sodomy, pornography, blackmail, theft, lying, adultery and blasphemy. These sins are broadcasted across the airwaves without shame into our homes, where they are viewed without conviction. We teach our children that these sins are wrong then in a deluded state of mind watch this garbage for entertainment. As a result, divorce, sexually transmitted diseases, drugs, teen pregnancy, abortion, suicide, and school shootings are widespread. Man has distorted God's perfect plan of one man for one woman in wedlock for life. Babies which are a blessing from the Lord, the fruit of the womb, have become refuse in the minds of those who fight for choice rather than life. Smoking ban commercials are advertised to help protect the unborn by the very same people who insist that the right of a woman to abort must be protected. This sort of irrational thinking can be found even in the minds of self professing "Christians." Many of these Christians believe that if they are good enough in this life and harm no-one their good works will outweigh their bad and by their own moral boot straps they will somehow be able to manufacture their own salvation. The knowledge of why Jesus Christ had to die on the cross has become lost in a sea of fable opinions and new age propaganda. The reasoning of many can be compared with the application of a bandage on a gangrene wound. Although the bandage may cover the wound itself the stench of puss from the infection will seep through leaving only one alternative, amputation. Likewise, when we stand before a perfect and Holy God at the final judgment, our opinions will be cast into the shadow of our sins. This will leave God with no other choice than to cut us off from entering heaven. God saw how great man's wickedness had become on the earth, every inclination of the thoughts of his heart was only evil all the time. So the conditions were the same in the days of Lot as they were at the time of Noah, and so it shall be in the latter days before the second coming of Christ.

Luke 17:26 - 30
And as it was in the days of Noah, so shall it be also in the days of the Son of man. They did eat, they drank, they married wives, they were given in marriage, until the day that Noah entered into the ark, and the flood came, and destroyed them all. Likewise also as it was in the days of Lot; they did eat, they drank, they bought, they sold, they planted, they builded; But the same day that Lot went out of Sodom it rained fire and brimstone from heaven, and destroyed *them* all. Even thus shall it be in the day when the Son of man is revealed. **KJV**

2 Timothy 3:1 - 5
But know this, that in the last days perilous times will come: For men will be lovers of themselves, lovers of money, boasters, proud, blasphemers, disobedient to parents, unthankful, unholy, unloving, unforgiving, slanderers, without self-control, brutal, despisers of good, traitors, headstrong, haughty, lovers of pleasure rather than lovers of God, having a form of godliness but denying its power. And from such people turn away! **NKJV**

2 Peter 3:3 - 7
Knowing this first, that there shall come in the last days scoffers, walking after their own lusts, And saying, Where is the promise of his coming? for since the fathers fell asleep, all things continue as *they were* from the beginning of the creation. For this they willingly are ignorant of, that by the word of God the heavens were of old, and the earth standing out of the water and in the water: Whereby the world that then was, being overflowed with water, perished. But the heavens and the earth, which are now, by the same word are kept in store, reserved unto fire against the day of judgment and perdition of ungodly men. **KJV**

15. Environmental Devastation Foretold

At the beginning of creation God gave to man dominion over the earth and the responsibility of being a good steward of the world's resources. However, man in his fallen condition has forgotten that he is to be a caretaker and instead has become a waster of the earth's resources. Through wars and greed it would be true to say that our generation has caused more destruction to the earth's environment than any previous generation in history. Man's greed in ravaging the planets resources and having no consideration for future generations is having a major effect on our planet. Atmospheric carbon dioxide is increasing dramatically due to the burning of fossil fuels which is destroying the earth's biosphere. As a result, thousands of animal, bird and fish species are dying each year. The planet is also battling global warming due to the depletion of the ozone layer. With an increase in high temperatures the threat of melting polar ice-caps and rising sea levels is striking fear into the hearts of many. Melanoma, the most dangerous form of skin cancer is causing serious illness and even death among millions around the globe from over exposure to harmful ultraviolet rays from the sun.

In the last one hundred years there has been a serious increase in chaotic weather including major floods, hurricanes, cyclones, and severe wild fires resulting from some of the worst droughts and heat waves ever recorded. In 2004, the Indian Ocean earthquake which had a magnitude of 9.15 triggered a serious of lethal tsunamis. Nearly a quarter of a million people died as a result, making it the deadliest tsunami in history. In 2005 Hurricane Katrina went on record as being one of the most deadliest and costly hurricanes in U.S. history causing $81.2 billion in damages. Environmentalists are fighting a losing battle to save the planet from total destruction. Some are even blaming population growth for many of the world's problems. But the earth's problem is not the growing population but mankind's sinful self-absorption of the earth's resources. All these environmental hazards fit in exactly with the end time predictions in the bible. The apostle Luke also records disturbances in the cosmos, pointing to signs in the sun, moon and stars preceding Christ's second coming. Perhaps panic will grip many because of the heavenly bodies on a near-collision course with the earth. This could well be an asteroid which might cause the earth to be tilted off its axis producing some of the largest tidal waves in history. In the book of Revelation the apostle John warns of God's coming judgment against all those who are responsible for contributing toward the planet's destruction.

Isaiah 51:6
Lift up your eyes to the heavens, and look upon the earth beneath: for the heavens shall vanish away like smoke, and the earth shall wax old like a garment, and they that dwell therein shall die in like manner: but my salvation shall be forever, and my righteousness shall not be abolished. **KJV**

Luke 21:25 - 27

"And there will be signs in the sun, in the moon, and in the stars; and on the earth distress of nations, with perplexity, the sea and the waves roaring; men's hearts failing them from fear and the expectation of those things which are coming on the earth, for the powers of the heavens will be shaken. Then they will see the Son of Man coming in a cloud with power and great glory." **NKJV**

Revelation 8:8 - 9

And the second angel sounded, and as it were a great mountain burning with fire was cast into the sea: and the third part of the sea became blood; And the third part of the creatures which were in the sea, and had life, died; and the third part of the ships were destroyed. **KJV**

Revelation 11:18

"The nations were angry, and Your wrath has come, And the time of the dead, that they should be judged, And that You should reward Your servants the prophets and the saints, And those who fear Your name, small and great, And should destroy those who destroy the earth." **NKJV**

Revelation 16:8 - 9

And the forth angel poured out his vial upon the sun; and power was given unto him to scorch men with fire. And men were scorched with great heat, and blasphemed the name of God, which hath power over these plagues: and they repented not to give him glory. **KJV**

CONCLUSION

To the one who accepts bible prophecy it is exciting to pick up a daily newspaper and compare what is happening in our world today with prophecies that were recorded thousands of years ago. No human psychic could have precisely foretold all of the remarkable signs and wonders above unless they were receiving direct revelation from God. So why does God reveal the future to us by giving us all these warning signs? One important reason is because He loves us and wants no one to perish without expressing faith in His beloved Son Jesus Christ. The future is revealed to us so that each one of us can personally repent of our sins and change our ways by trusting in the saviour and avoid God's coming wrath upon mankind.

From a Christian perspective we do not worship an absentee God but a God who is very much in control of these world shaping events. As Christians we are not to be disturbed by the chaos, violence, bloodshed, strife and the threat of war that fills our television screens and daily newspapers. We know that what is happening in the world today is a consequence of man's sin and greed and we know what the future holds for planet earth. God allows us to know what is coming upon the earth to motivate us to make the changes we need to make in our lives before Christ returns. The bible says that there is a day coming when God will reveal His righteous judgment against all ungodly and unrighteous men. Those who have suppressed and substituted the truth of God's word with preconceived ideas from their own imaginations will have done so at the expense of their souls. Let us not be found in ignorance by the Lord on His return, instead let us hold fast to the truth which He has provided us with in His word. God is the only one to have power over life and death, so having reverence for Him should be our main priority in life.

Ecclesiastes 12:13 - 14
Let us hear the conclusion of the whole matter: fear God and keep His commandments, for this is man's all. For God will bring every work into judgment, Including every secret thing, Whether good or evil. **NKJV**

Luke 21:28
And when these things begin to come to pass, then look up, and lift up your heads; for your redemption draweth nigh. **KJV**

2 Peter 1:19
We have also a more sure word of prophecy; whereunto ye do well that ye take heed, as unto a light that shineth in a dark place, until the day dawn, and the day star arise in your hearts. **KJV**

FURTHER READING

Chapter 1 - Bible questions and answers

1. Why do I need to be Born Again?
See also, (Jeremiah 17:9) (Matthew 19:5) (Mark 7:21 - 23, 10:6 - 7) (Romans 1:22 - 27) (1 Corinthians 15:45) (Ephesians 2:3, 5:31) (Hebrews 4:14 - 16, 9:27) (1 John 2:2, 3:8)

2. What does it mean to be Born Again?
See also, (John 10:27 - 30) (1 Corinthians 3:16, 6:11, 19 - 20) (2 Corinthians 1:22) (Galatians 5:17) (Ephesians 1:3 - 5, 4:17 - 23, 30) (Colossians 1:28) (Hebrews 12:23) (1 Peter 1:4 - 5) (1 John 4:13, 5:3)

3. Do Good Works help you to earn your Salvation?
See also, (Habakkuk 2:4) (Mark 10:17 - 22) (Luke 10:20) (John 17:3, 9) (Romans 1:17, 3:20 - 28, 4:6, 13, 16, 5:1 - 2, 9:11, 30) (2 Corinthians 1:24) (Galatians 3:6 - 13, 24 - 26) (Philippians 3:9, 4:3) (Hebrews 10:5, 38 - 39, 12:23) (1 John 1:8 - 9)

4. Who Should I Pray to?
See also, (Luke 4:8, 11:1 - 4) (John 16:26) (1 Timothy 2:8) (1 Peter 2:22) (James 5:15 - 16) (1 John 2:1)

5. Who Should I Trust in for My Salvation?
See also, (2 Corinthians 6:2) (Colossians 2:13 - 15) (2 Timothy 2:1) (Hebrews 2:3, 5:9, 9:22) (1 Peter 2:6) (1 John 2:12, 3:5)

6. Is Baptism Necessary for Salvation?
See also, (John 4:1 - 2, 8:46) (Romans 6:5 - 11, 8:1 - 11) (1 Corinthians 6:11) (Galatians 2:20)

7. Is the Bible's Interpretation Limited to Only One True Church?
See also, (Jeremiah 17:5) (Psalm 1:2, 119:9, 105, 130) (Matthew 11:25) (Acts 17:11, 28:25) (Romans 12:3 - 8) (2 Corinthians 1:3, 13:5) (Galatians 1:11 - 12, 3:2) (Colossians 3:16) (Hebrews 3:7 - 8, 10:15 - 16) (1 Peter 3:15)

8. Who is the Head of the Church

See also, (Deuteronomy 32:4, 15) (1 Samuel 2:2) (Psalm 62:1 - 2) (Isaiah 50:4) (Matthew 18:4, 19) (Mark 1:30, 9:38 - 40) (Luke 22:24 - 27) (John 1:42) (Acts 14:23 (Romans 9:33, 15:4) (1 Corinthians 1:2) (Galatians 2:11 - 13) (Ephesians 5:24 - 25) (Colossians 2:19) (Hebrews 5:12) (1 Peter 2:4 - 5) (3 John 9 - 10)

9. Does Purgatory Exist?

See also, (Psalm 49:7, 103:12) (Isaiah 66:15) (Malachi 3:2) (Luke 16:19 - 31) (John 19:30) (Romans 3:24 - 27, 5:18, 8:1, 30 - 39) (1 Corinthians 6:20, 7:23) (2 Corinthians 5:10) (Ephesians 2:18, 4:14) (Colossians 1:20, 2:13 - 14) (Hebrews 9:12, 12:23) (1 Peter 2:10, 3:18) (2 Peter 1:9, 18 - 19, 2:1, 3:18) (1 John 1:7) (Revelation 1:14, 5:9)

Further Reading online

Understanding Roman Catholicism; Rick Jones http://www.chick.com/reading/books/160/160cont.asp

Answers to my catholic friends; Thomas F. Heinze http://www.chick.com/reading/books/218/218cont.asp

Chapter 2 - Scientific Facts in the Bible

5. Mountains and Valleys at the Bottom of the Ocean

See also, (Psalm 18:6) (Matthew 16:4) (Ephesians 4:8 - 9)
http://creation.com/jonah-and-the-great-fish
http://www.answersingenesis.org/articles/am/v1/n1/great-fish

7. The Bible and the Spreading of Disease

See also, (Leviticus 14:5, 15:11 - 12)

13. The Bible and Dinosaurs

See also, (Exodus 20:11, 31:17) (Hebrews 4:4)
http://www.apologeticspress.org/articles/3626

Chapter 3 - Manuscript Evidence

See also, (Luke 1:2 - 3, 24:48) (John 19:35) (Acts 1:8) (1 Corinthians 9:1, 15:4 - 8) (Hebrews 12:1)

Chapter 4 - The Life of Jesus Foretold Through Prophecy

Introduction
See also, (Luke 24:27) (Acts 3:18, 8:32 - 35, 28:23) (Hebrews 1:1 - 2)

Prophecies Concerning Jesus Life, Ministry and Resurrection

1. Born of the Seed of Woman
See also, (Romans 16:20) (Matthew 8:31) (Romans 8:20 - 21) (Revelations 21:4 - 5) (Hebrews 2:14 - 15)

2. Born of a Virgin
See also, (Genesis 4:1) (Psalm 69:8) (Matthew 1:25, 12:46, 13:55 - 56) (Mark 6:3) (Luke 1:36, 2:42 - 43) (John 2:12, 7:3, 5) (Acts 1:14) (1 Corinthians 9:5) (Galatians 1:19) (Colossians 4:10) (1 Timothy 4:1 - 5) (Matthew 1:23)

3. Born in Bethlehem
See also, (John 6:48) (Matthew 2:1 - 4) (John 7:42)

4. Preceded by a Messenger
See also, (Isaiah 40:3 - 4) (Matthew 3:1 - 3, 11:10) (John 1:23)

5. Enter Jerusalem on a Donkey
See also, (Numbers 19:2) (Deuteronomy 21:3) (1 Samuel 6:7) (Matthew 21:7 - 9)

6. Perform Miracles
See also, (Luke 4:17 - 19, 17:12 - 19) (Matthew 9:35) (Mark 7:33 - 35) (John 5:5 - 9)

7. Saviour to both Jews and Gentiles
See also, (Isaiah 60:3) (Luke 2:32) (Genesis 3:8) (John 1:1 - 3) (Colossians 1:16) (1 Peter 1:20)

8. Shall be Judge
See also, (Isaiah 33:22) (Micah 4:1 - 3) (Acts 26:23) (John 5:22) (2 Corinthians 5:10) (1 Timothy 4:1) (Revelations 20:15)

9. Raised from the Dead
(Matthew 28:19) (Mark 16:15 - 16) (Luke 5:21, 24:47) (John 20:23) (2 Peter 2:4) (Matthew 28:6) (Ephesians 4:9) (Hebrews 9:12) (1 Peter 3:19)

10. Ascension into Heaven
See also, (Psalm 110:1) (Colossians 3:1) (Hebrews 1:3, 10:12 - 14)

Prophecies fulfilled in one twenty-four hour period

1. Betrayed by a Friend
See also, (2 Samuel 17:23) (Matthew 26:49 - 50)

3. Silver to be thrown into God's House 4. Silver Used to buy Potter's Field
See also, (2 Corinthians 7:10)

5. Forsaken by His Disciples
See also, (Matthew 26:31)

7. Silent before His Accusers
See also, (Acts 8:26 - 40)

8. Wounded and Bruised
See also, (1 Peter 2:24)

9. He Was Hated Without Cause
See also, (Isaiah 49:7) (Matthew 10:22) (John 3:19, 15:18, 17:14)

10. Struck and Spat Upon
See also, (Micah 5:1) (John 19:3) (Luke 22:63)

11. Mocked and Ridiculed
See also, (2 Peter 3:4 - 9) (Matthew 7:13) (Matthew 27:41 - 43) (Luke 23:35)

12. People Would Shake Their Heads at Him
See also, (John 5:24, 6:47, 8:24) (Acts 13:38 - 39) (Mark 15:29)

14. He Would Fall Under The Cross
See also, (Mark 15:21) (Luke 23: 26)

15. Executed With Thieves
See also, (Matthew 27:44) (Mark 15:32) (Luke 23:42 - 43) (Mark 15:27 - 28)

16. They Pierced His Hands and Feet
See also, (Zechariah 12:10) (Deuteronomy 21:23) (John 20:25)

17. Pray for His Persecutors
See also, (Hebrews 9:15) (John14:6)

18. His Friends and Family Stood Afar Off
See also, (John 2:3 - 4, 19:26 - 27) (Matthew 17:5) (Matthew 27:55, 56) (Mark 15:40)

20. He Would Suffer Thirst 21. Gall and Vinegar Would be Offered to Him
See also, (Matthew 27:34, 48)

22. Forsaken by God
See also, (Romans 5:8)

23. Commit Himself to God
See also, (Luke 10:20) (Philippians 4:3) (Hebrews 1:3, 8:1 - 2, 9:11 - 15, 22, 10:18, 12:23) (Acts 17:24 - 25)

24. His Bones Would Remain Unbroken
See also, (Exodus 12:46) (Psalm 22:14)

25. Darkness over the Land
See also, (Matthew 27:51 - 54) (Mark 15:25)

26. His Side Would Be Pierced 27. His Heart Would Be Broken
See also, (Psalm 22:14)

29. Rejected by His Own People
See also, (Psalm 22:6) (Matthew 21:42) (John 1:11)

Chapter 5 - Bible Prophecy and the Occult

See also, (Leviticus 20:6, 27) (Deuteronomy 13:1 - 3, 18:9 - 22) (1 Samuel 28:3)
(1 Chronicles 10:13) (2 Chronicles 33:6) (Daniel 2:28) (Malachi 3:5) (Mark 5:2
- 13) (Luke 4:17 - 21) (John 4:17 - 19, 13:19) (Acts 16:16 - 19) (1 Corinthians
12:10) (Galatians 5:19 - 21) (Ephesians 6:12) (1 Timothy 4:1 - 3) (2 Peter 1:20 -
21) (1 John 4:1 - 3) (Revelations 21:8)

Chapter 6 - End Time Prophecies

4. The Rebirth of Israel and the Regathering of the Jews
See also, (Genesis 15:18, 17:7 - 8) (Deuteronomy 4:40) (Malachi 3:12)

5. Jerusalem a Cup of Trembling
See also, (Joel 3:9 - 14)

7. Israel Shall Blossom and Bud
See also, (Leviticus 19:23) (Jeremiah 1:11 - 12) (Isaiah 55:12)

9. The East Gate Sealed until Christ's Second Coming
See also, (Psalm 118:25 - 26) (Zechariah 9:9) (Matthew 21:9 - 13)

10. The Rebuilding of the Third Temple in Jerusalem
See also, (Ezekiel 36:25 - 26)

12. Environmental Devastation Foretold
See also, (Revelation 6:12 - 14)

14. The Revived Roman Empire
See also, (Daniel chapter two) (Revelation 13:1 - 8)
http://www.raptureready.com/abc/Roman_Empire.html

15. Moral Decline and Blasphemy
See also, (Genesis 6:1 - 12) (Psalm 127:3) (Ezekiel 16:49 - 50) (Matthew 7:13 - 14)
(Jude 1:6 - 7)
http://www.raptureready.com/abc/abc.html

Recommended Viewing Online

http://freehovind.com/watch
http://www.answersingenesis.org/media/video/ondemand

Relentless; The Struggle for Peace in the Middle East www.balfourbooks.net
http://video.google.com/videoplay?docid=-2533702461706761547#

Israel, Islam and Armageddon;
http://video.google.com/videosearch?q=catholicism+crisis+of+faith&emb=0#q
=Israel+and+aremgeddon&emb=0

Catholicism Crisis of Faith; www.Chick.com
http://video.google.com/videoplay?docid=-7116805989986440367#

Messages from Heaven; www.eternal-productions.org
http://www.youtube.com/watch?v=g6Nm6bXk9NQ

WEBSITES

www.answersingenesis.org
www.bethlehemstar.net
www.davidjeremiah.org
www.drdino.com
www.goodfight.org
www.intouch.org
www.israeltoday.co.il
www.narth.com
www.nephilimapocalypse.com/default.asp

www.onehumanrace.com
www.opendoors.co.uk
www.persecution.com
www.persecution.org
www.rldbooks.org
www.rzim.org
www.templeinstitute.org

Books

Cahill, M., One Thing You Can't Do In Heaven, 2006
Coffey, T., Once a Catholic, 1993
Comfort, R., The Evidence Bible, 2004
Gumbel, N., Alpha Questions of Life, 2003
Ham, K., The New Answers Book, 2007
Ham, K., The Great Dinosaur Mystery Solved, 2000
Ham, K., The Lie Evolution, 2001
Heron, P., The Nephilim and the Pyramid of the Apocalypse, 2004
Hunt, D., A Woman Rides the Beast, 1994
Jack, V., Believe and be Baptised, 1986
Jeffrey, G., The Signature of God, 1998
Jeffrey, G., The New Temple and the Second Coming, 2007
Jeffrey, G., Armageddon Appointment with Destiny, 1990
Jeffrey, G., Countdown to the Apocalypse, 2008
Jeremiah, D., What in the World is Going On?, 2008
Kendall, R.T., Once Saved, Always Saved, 2001
Lahaye, T.
Hindson, E., The Popular Bible Prophecy Commentary, 2007
Mac Donald, W., Believer's Bible Commentary, 1995
Mc Dowell, J., Evidence that demands a Verdict (New and Revised) 1999
Morris, H. Dr., The New Defender's study Bible, 2006
Sarfati, J.D., Refuting Evolution, 1999
Sarfati, J.D., Refuting Evolution 2, 2002
Strobel, L., The Case for Christ, 1998
Watchman, N., The Normal Christian Life, 1977

Glossary

Accumulate	To gather or collect, often in gradual degrees
Affirmation	The act or an instance of affirming; state of being affirmed. The assertion that something exists or is true
Anatomist	A specialist in anatomy
Ancestral	Having to do with or inherited from an ancestor or ancestors; their ancestral home.
Anti-Semitism	Discrimination against or prejudice or hostility toward Jews
Appraisal	The act of estimating or judging the nature or value of something or someone
Archaeologist	The scientific study of historic or peoples and their cultures by analysis of their artifacts, inscriptions, monuments, and other such remains, esp. those that have been excavated
Ascension	The bodily ascending of Christ from earth to heaven
Asphyxiation	To cause to die or lose consciousness by impairing normal breathing, as by gas or other noxious agents, choke, suffocate, smother
Assimilated	To conform or adjust to the customs, attitudes, etc. of a group or nation
Assumption	Something taken for granted, a supposition, a correct assumption
Atonement	The doctrine concerning the reconciliation of God and humankind, esp. as accomplished through the life, suffering and death of Christ
Attributed	To regard as resulting from a specified cause, consider as caused by something indicated (usually fol. by to) She attributed his bad temper to ill health

Authenticity	The quality of being authentic, genuineness
Biometrics	The measurement of physical characteristics, voice or fingerprints, DNA, or retinal patterns, for use in verifying the identity of individuals. This technology can be used to define an individual's unique identity
Blasphemy	To speak impiously or irreverently of God
Cataclysmic	Of the nature of, or having the effect of, a cataclysm, cataclysmic changes
Characteristic	A distinguishing feature or quality
Communion	The partaking of the bread and wine in remembrance of Jesus Christ's sacrifice for sins, His resurrection and the second coming
Condemn	To pronounce to be guilty, sentence to punishment, to condemn a murderer to life imprisonment
Consummation	An ultimate goal or end. Sense of "completion of a marriage (by sexual intercourse)"
Corroborating	To make more certain; confirm. Verify, authenticate, support or validate
Crusade	Any of the military expeditions undertaken by the Christians of Europe in the 11th, 12th and 13th centuries for the recovery of the Holy Land from the Muslims
Decomposition	The state of being decomposed, decay
Deity	Divine character or nature, esp. that of the Supreme Being, divinity
Denominations	A religious group, usually including many local churches
Desolate	Deprived or destitute of inhabitants, deserted or uninhabited
Despicable	Deserving to be despised or contemptible

Diaphragm	A muscular membranous partition separating the abdominal and thoracic cavities and functioning in respiration. Also called midriff
Dogma	A system of principles or beliefs as of a church
Dogmas	A specific tenet or doctrine authoritatively laid down, as by a church
Elders	A person who is older or higher in rank than oneself, often assisting the pastor in services
Eunuch	A castrated man employed to attend a king's concubines or wives
Evolutionist	A person who believes in or supports a theory of evolution, esp. in biology
Exclusive	Not admitting of something else, incompatible. Single or sole
Expiate	To atone for; make amends or reparation for, to expiate one's crimes
Expulsion	The act of driving out or expelling
Figurative	Of the nature of or involving a figure of speech, esp. a metaphor metaphorical, not literal, a figurative expression
Fundamental	Serving as, or being an essential part of, a foundation or basis. A basic rule or principle. The strict following of the fundamental doctrines of any religion or system of thought.
Genocidal	The deliberate and systematic extermination of a national, racial, political or cultural group.
Gentiles	Meaning in general all nations except the Jews
Geophysical	The branch of geology that deals with the physics of the earth and its atmosphere including oceanography, seismology, volcanology and geomagnetism

Heathen	An unconverted individual of a people that do not acknowledge the God of the bible
Heretic	A professed believer who maintains religious opinions contrary to those accepted by his or her church or rejects doctrines prescribed by that church
Hydrography	The science of the measurement, description, and mapping of the surface waters of the earth, with special reference to their use for navigation
Indiscernible	Not discernible, that cannot be seen or perceived clearly, imperceptible
Infallible	Immune from fallacy or liability to error in expounding matters of faith or morals
Iniquity	Gross injustice or wickedness. A violation of right or duty, wicked act or sin
Innumerable	Incapable of being counted, countless
Irrefutable	Indisputable, incontrovertible, undeniable
Justified	To declare innocent or guiltless, absolve or acquit
Kosher	Conforming to dietary laws, ritually pure, kosher meat
Manuscript	The original text of an author's work, handwritten or now usually typed, that is submitted to a publisher
Mediator	A person who mediates, esp. between parties and variance
Messiah	God's anointed one, Christ Jesus
Meteorology	The science dealing with the atmosphere and its phenomena, including weather and climate
Methodology	A set or system of methods, principles, and rules for regulating a given discipline, as in the arts or sciences

Ministering	To attend to the wants and needs of others
Obligation	Something by which a person is bound or obliged to do certain things
Oceanography	The exploration and scientific study of the ocean and its phenomena. Also called oceanology
Paleontology	The scientific study of life in the geologic past, especially through the study of animal and plant fossils
Papyrologists	The study of papyrus manuscripts
Paralysis	Loss or impairment of the ability to move a body part, usually as a result of damage to its nerve supply
Persecuted	To pursue with harassing or oppressive treatment, esp. because of religion, race or beliefs
Petroglyph	A drawing or carving on rock
Pharisees	A member of a Jewish sect that flourished during the 1st century B.C. and 1st century A.D. Pharisees adhered to oral laws and traditions and a belief in an afterlife and the coming of the Messiah.
Pictograph	A record consisting of pictorial symbols, as a cave drawing
Pilgrimage	A journey, esp. a long one, made to some sacred place as an act of religious devotion
Preappointed	To appoint beforehand
Pre-eminence	The state or character of being preeminent, to excel far above
Prophecy	The foretelling or prediction of what is to come. A divinely inspired utterance or revelation

Propitiatory	Propitiation is a theological term denoting that by which God is rendered propitious, i.e., that 'satisfaction' or 'appeasement' by which it becomes consistent with His character and government to pardon and bless sinners. The act of atoning for sin or wrongdoing. The act of delivering from sin or saving from evil. Something done or paid in expiation of a wrong
Prothrombin	A plasma protein involved in blood coagulation that on activation by factors in the plasma is converted to Thrombin, an enzyme of the blood plasma that catalyzes the conversion of fibrinogen to fibrin, the last step of the blood clotting process
Providentially	Pertaining to or resulting from divine providence, providential care
Rabbi	A title of respect for a Jewish scholar or teacher
Reconciliation	An act of reconciling or the state of being reconciled
Repentance	Deep sorrow, contrition for a past sin or wrongdoing
Repetition	The act of repeating, repeated action or performance
Resurrection	The act of rising from the dead
Righteousness	The quality or state of being just or rightful
Sacrificial	Pertaining to or concerned with sacrifice
Salvation	Deliverance from the power and penalty of sin, redemption
Scripture	The sacred writings of the Old and New Testament
Simultaneously	Existing, occurring, or operating at the same time
Stigmata	Bodily marks, sores, or sensations of pain corresponding in location to the crucifixion wounds of Jesus. Marks resembling the wounds of the crucified body of Christ

Subsequent   Following in order or succession, succeeding, a subsequent section in a treaty

Substitutionary   A person serving in the place of another, a substitute

Synagogue   A Jewish house of worship, often having facilities for religious instruction

Temptation   Something that tempts, entices or allures

Tribulation   The tribulation indicates a definite period spoken of by the Lord in in (Matthew 24:15, Mark 13:14, with Daniel 11:31; 12:11) where the time is mentioned as preceding His Second Coming and as a period in which the Jewish nation, restored to Palestine in unbelief by Gentile instrumentality, will suffer an unprecedented outburst of fury on the part of the antichristian powers confederate under the Man of Sin.

Unregenerate   Not regenerate, not renewed in heart and mind or reborn in spirit, unrepentant

Vindicate   To clear, as from an accuation, imputation, suspicion, or the like, to vindicate someone's honor